IGNITED

AIR FRYER TOASTER OVEN

COOKBOOK FOR BEGINNERS

1000-DAY ALL-INCLUSIVE AND MOUTHWATERING RECIPES PERFECT FOR A HEALTHY AND PLEASURABLE EATING

MARIA RIDGE

CONTENTS

INTRODUCTION

How Does Air Frying Work?

Ever wonder why fried mozzarella sticks and potato chips get crunchy? All that hot oil causes the surface water in food to boil super-quick and exit as steam — leaving the outside of your food dry, which is the perfect setup for golden brown, crispy results.

Air fryers are full of hot air, literally. Air replaces oil in this machine and crisps and browns while it circulates around food. Air fried foods generally have less fat and calories per serving compared to their doppelganger fried version.

Seeing the Benefits of the ignited Air Fryer Oven

1. Protect the food's nutrients

Unlike deep frying, Air Fryers do not deconstruct the food's good nutrients and add on bad fats. If you think your yasai tempura (deep-fried battered vegetables) are healthy, here is news for you; while they may look like they are full of nutritious elements, the deep frying process would have destroyed the beneficial vitamins and minerals contained in the vegetables.

2. Keeping cancer at bay

For some oils (e.g. olive and flax seed), their chemical structure changes in high heat causing them to transform into bad forms of fat. Additionally, since there is little oil used, there is little chance for food to produce carcinogens that activate cancer cells.

3. Calories are good, but too much spells trouble!

Fried foods are high in calories which is the leading cause of weight gain and obesity. Obesity will then lead to a plethora of killer diseases such as diabetes, cancer, stroke, sleep problems, and immobility to name a few. Adopting a low-fat diet will help you maintain your weight or prevent weight loss because essentially, you are eating fewer calories. Therefore, eating Air Fryer-cooked food will support your weight loss journey.

4. Build a fortress for your heart

Eating food fried with an Air Fryer reduces the risk of heart diseases and protects your body by helping you absorb the necessary nutrients. Since a minimal amount of oil is used to prepare food, you can be sure that your body will not accumulate excessive fats in the long run. Instead, the optimal amount of oil used will help your body protect your heart.

5. Keeping your kidneys clear

Consuming excess amounts of deep-fried food will impair your kidney's ability to filter our harmful fats. Therefore, eating food fried by an Air Fryer can help you lower your risks of getting kidney disease. If you are finding it difficult to quit deep-fried food cold turkey, using an Air Fryer will ease your transition to a healthier diet.

6. Reduce the worries of fat

Fat is a macro nutrient – it is essential to help control inflammation, blood clotting, maintaining healthy hair and skin, prevent heart diseases, provide energy and assist in the absorption of vitamins A, D, E, and K. While it is important to your bodily functions, too much of it is detrimental to health. An Air Fryer is a modern kitchen appliance that fries food using heated hot air by using at most a tablespoon of oil. This way, you are able to eat fried food without worrying about the negative effects of fatty food on your health.

Tricks on How to Use the Accessories of the ignited Air Fryer Oven

1. Heating Element Protection Cover

The protection cover can prevent the food from contacting the heating element.

Let the side with wire handle face down, slide along the top plastic shelf near the heating element in the oven to install the protection cover. Take out the protection cover by pulling the wire handle.

2. Air Flow Racks

The air flow racks can be used not only for dehydration but also to cook crispy snacks or reheat foods like pizza.

Slide along the rack shelf to install or take out the air flow racks.

3. Rotisserie Fork Set

The rotisserie fork set is used for roasting large meat or whole chicken.

Install a fork backwards to the gear on the shaft. Force shaft lengthwise through meat/chicken in center. Install another fork towards the meat/chicken. Slide both forks into meat/chicken and adjust the meat/chicken to the middle of the shaft, then drive the screws to lock the forks in position.

You can adjust the forks closer to the middle if needed but never outwards to the groove of both ends.

To install the rotisserie fork set, let the end with the gear face towards left, insert the grooves on both ends of the shaft into the rotating shelf.

4. Rotisserie Basket

Great for fries, roasting nuts and other snacks.

Use the hasp to open and lock the rotisserie basket. To install the rotisserie basket, let the the gear face towards left, insert the grooves on both ends of the shaft into the rotating shelf.

5. Fetch Tool

Used to remove the rotisserie basket or fork set from the appliance.

Place the fetch tool under the shaft at both side of the rotisserie basket or fork set，then gently extract the rotisserie basket or fork set out.

6. Drip Tray

Cook with the drip tray for easy clean ups.

Put the drip tray into the bottom of the appliance when in use. It is easy to take out for cleaning.

7. Door

The door is detachable for easy cleaning.

Open the door at a 30°angle from the appliance and gently put on or take off the door.

The appliance will not work with the door open

- To keep your air fryer oven in good working order, make sure to remove all food residues and grease splatters from interior surfaces on a regular basis. Regular cleaning will also reduce the fire hazard risk.
- ➢ Unplug the air fryer oven from the power supply. Allow the appliance to cool.
- ➢ Remove all accessories (crumb tray, oven rack, food tray, air-frying basket, pizza pan) from the oven cavity.

Interior walls and oven door

- ➢ Use a damp cloth and mild detergent solution on a sponge to clean the interior walls and door of the air fryer oven. Repeat with a dry, clean cloth.
- ➢ Never use harsh abrasives, corrosive products or as these could damage the oven surface. Never use steel wool pads or other abrasive cleaning products. Abrasive cleaners, scrubbing brushes and chemical cleaners will damage the coating on this unit. Pieces can break off the and touch electrical parts involving a risk of electrical shock.
- ➢ If scrubbing is necessary, use a nonabrasive nylon or polyester mesh pad.

Crumb tray

- ➢ To remove crumbs and drippings from the bottom of the oven, slide out the crumb tray and discard any crumbs. Wipe the crumb tray clean and replace. To remove baked-on grease, soak the tray in hot, sudsy water or use nonabrasive cleaners. Never operate the oven without the crumb tray in place!

Exterior surfaces

- ➢ Wipe the appliance housing clean with a damp cloth and a mild detergent. Apply the cleansing agent to the cloth, not directly onto the oven. Dry thoroughly

BREAKFAST

Baked Steel-cut Oatmeal

Servings: 2
Cooking Time: 60 Minutes

Ingredients:

- ½ cup steel-cut oats
- 1 tablespoon unsalted butter, cut into 2 pieces
- 2 cups boiling water, plus extra as needed
- ⅛ teaspoon table salt

Directions:

1. Adjust toaster oven rack to middle position and preheat the toaster oven to 450 degrees. Place oats and butter in 8-inch square baking dish or pan and bake until oats are golden brown and fragrant, 5 to 7 minutes, stirring thoroughly halfway through baking to incorporate butter into oats.

2. Remove pan from oven and reduce oven temperature to 325 degrees. Carefully stir boiling water and salt into oats and bake until oats are softened but still retain some chew and mixture thickens and resembles warm pudding, 40 to 45 minutes, rotating pan halfway through baking. Remove pan from oven, cover, and let sit for 5 minutes. Stir oatmeal to recombine and adjust consistency with extra boiling water as needed. Serve.

Salmon Burgers

Servings: 4
Cooking Time: 25 Minutes

Ingredients:

- ¾ cup Homemade Bread Crumbs
- 1 15-ounce can salmon, drained
- 1 small zucchini, finely chopped
- 2 tablespoons finely chopped onions
- 1 egg
- 1 teaspoon dried rosemary
- 1 teaspoon lemon juice
- 1 teaspoon garlic powder
- Salt and freshly ground black pepper to taste
- 1 teaspoon vegetable oil

Directions:

1. Preheat the toaster oven to 400° F.
2. Blend all ingredients except the oil and form patties 1½ inches thick. Place on an oiled or nonstick 8½ × 8½ × 2-inch square baking (cake) pan.
3. BAKE for 25 minutes, or until the patties are lightly browned.

French Toast Sticks

Servings: 4

Cooking Time: 8 Minutes

Ingredients:

- 2 eggs
- ¼ cup half-and-half
- ½ teaspoon vanilla extract
- 6 slices wheat bread, cut into 1-inch strips
- 1 teaspoon ground cinnamon
- 2 tablespoons granulated sugar
- Maple syrup or pureed strawberries for serving

Directions:

1. In an 8-x-12-inch casserole dish, whisk together the eggs, half-and-half, and vanilla. Lay the strips of bread into the baking dish and flip around. Allow the bread to soak up the egg mixture for 10 minutes.
2. Meanwhile, in a small bowl, stir together the cinnamon and sugar.
3. Place the soaked bread strips into the air fryer oven, not touching one another. Spray with cooking spray and sprinkle the cinnamon and sugar mixture onto the bread sticks.
4. Air fry the French toast sticks at 370°F for 8 minutes. Cook in batches, as needed.
5. Serve with maple syrup or pureed strawberries.

Paleo Spiced Zucchini Bread

Servings: 8

Cooking Time: 45 Minutes

Ingredients:
- Dry Ingredients
- 1½ cups almond flour
- 2 tablespoons coconut flour
- 1 teaspoon cinnamon
- ¼ teaspoon allspice
- ⅛ teaspoon ground cloves
- 1 teaspoon baking powder
- ½ teaspoon baking soda
- ¼ teaspoon salt
- 1 cup chopped walnuts
- Wet Ingredients
- ⅓ cup coconut sugar
- 1 teaspoon vanilla extract
- 3 large eggs
- 5 tablespoons olive oil
- 2 tablespoons applesauce
- 1 cup shredded zucchini, squeezed to remove excess moisture

Directions:
1. Stir together all the dry ingredients in a large bowl.
2. Whisk all the wet ingredients in a separate bowl.
3. Add the dry ingredients to the wet ingredients and stir to combine. Allow the batter to rest for 5 minutes. This allows the coconut flour to absorb the batter.
4. Preheat the toaster Oven to 350°F.
5. Grease the mini loaf pans with coconut oil spray. Divide the batter evenly between the pans.
6. Place the mini loaf pans on the wire rack, then insert the rack at mid position in the preheated oven.
7. Select the Bake function, adjust time to 45 minutes, and press Start/Pause.
8. Remove when a toothpick or cake tester inserted into the middle comes out clean.
9. Remove zucchini bread from the pans and place on a cooling rack for 15 minutes before slicing.

Morning Glory Muffins

Servings: 6

Cooking Time: 25 Minutes

Ingredients:

- Oil spray (hand-pumped)
- ¼ cup raisins
- 1 cup whole-wheat flour
- ½ cup packed dark brown sugar
- 1 teaspoon baking soda
- 1¼ teaspoons pumpkin pie spice
- ¼ teaspoon sea salt
- 1 cup carrot, finely shredded
- 1 small apple, peeled, cored, and shredded
- ⅓ cup shredded, sweetened coconut
- 2 large eggs
- ¼ cup canola oil
- Juice and zest of ½ orange

Directions:

1. Place the rack on position 1 and preheat the toaster oven on BAKE to 350°F for 5 minutes. Lightly spray 6 muffin cups with the oil or line them with paper liners.
2. In a small bowl, cover the raisins with hot water and set aside.
3. In a large bowl, whisk the flour, brown sugar, baking soda, pumpkin pie spice, and salt. Add the carrot, apple, and coconut, and toss to mix.
4. In a small bowl, beat the eggs, oil, orange juice, and orange zest.
5. Drain the raisins, squeezing out as much water as possible.
6. Add the wet ingredients and raisins to the dry ingredients and mix until the batter is just combined.
7. Spoon the batter into the muffin cups.
8. Bake for 25 minutes or until a knife inserted in the center comes out clean.
9. Remove from the oven and let cool before serving.

Quick Fruit And Raisin Bread

Servings: 6

Cooking Time: 35 Minutes

Ingredients:

- 2 cups unbleached flour
- 3 tablespoons margarine
- 4 ¾ cup low-fat buttermilk
- 5 teaspoons baking powder
- 1 egg, beaten
- 2 tablespoons honey
- ¼ cup chopped raisins
- ½ cup chopped dried fruit
- 3 tablespoons chopped almonds
- 4 ½ teaspoon grated nutmeg
- Salt to taste

Directions:

1. Preheat the toaster oven to 400° F.
2. Combine all the ingredients in a large bowl, stirring well. Pour the batter into an oiled or nonstick regular-size 8½ × 4½ × ⅔-inch loaf pan or 2 small-size 3½ × 7½ × 2¼-inch loaf pans.
3. BAKE for 35 minutes, or until a toothpick inserted in the center comes out clean.

Granola With Sesame And Sunflower Seeds

Servings: 4
Cooking Time: 20 Minutes

Ingredients:
- 2 cups rolled oats
- ½ cup sunflower seeds
- ½ cup sesame seeds
- ½ cup unsweetened shredded
- Coconut
- ½ cup slivered almonds
- ½ cup honey
- 1 tablespoon vegetable oil
- 1 teaspoon toasted sesame oil
- 1 teaspoon ground cinnamon
- Pinch of grated nutmeg
- Salt to taste

Directions:
1. Preheat the toaster oven to 375° F.
2. Combine all the granola ingredients in a large bowl, mixing well.
3. Spread the mixture evenly in an oiled or nonstick 6½ × 6½ × 2-inch square (cake) pan.
4. BAKE for 20 minutes, turning the ingredients every 5 minutes with tongs to toast evenly. Cool and store in an airtight container in the refrigerator.

Grilled Dagwood

Servings: 4

Cooking Time: 20 Minutes

Ingredients:

- 4 slices whole wheat or multigrain bread
- 1 tablespoon Dijon mustard
- 2 tablespoons fresh or canned bean sprouts, washed and well drained
- 2 tablespoons chopped watercress
- 2 tablespoons chopped roasted pimientos
- 3 slices reduced-fat Swiss cheese
- 2 slices low-fat honey ham
- 2 tablespoons garlic hummus
- 6 slices sweet pickle
- 4 slices low-fat smoked turkey
- 1 tablespoon Yogurt Cheese Spread (recipe follows)
- 1 tablespoon chopped Vidalia onion
- 1 tablespoon ketchup
- 1 tablespoon pitted and chopped black olives

Directions:

1. Preheat the toaster oven to 350° F.
2. Spread the first bread slice with ½ tablespoon Dijon mustard. Add 1 tablespoon sprouts, 1 tablespoon watercress, 1 tablespoon pimientos, 1 slice Swiss cheese, and 1 slice honey ham.
3. Spread the second bread slice with ½ tablespoon Dijon mustard, turn it over, and lay it on top of the first. Spread the other side of the second slice with 1 tablespoon hummus, 1 slice honey ham, 3 pickle slices, 1 tablespoon watercress, and 2 slices smoked turkey.
4. Spread the third bread slice with the Yogurt Cheese Spread, turn it over, and lay it on top of the second slice of bread. Spread the other side of the third slice with 1 tablespoon hummus and add the chopped onion, 1 tablespoon pimientos, 3 pickle slices, 1 slice Swiss cheese, and 2 slices smoked turkey.
5. Spread the fourth bread slice with the ketchup and add 1 tablespoon sprouts, 1 tablespoon pimientos, 1 slice Swiss cheese, and the black olives. Lift up all the other bread slices together and place this one on the bottom. Then put the slices together and wrap in aluminum foil so that the seam is on the top of the slices. Open the seam to expose the tops of the slices and place on the rack in the toaster oven, seam side up.
6. BAKE 20 minutes, or until the top is lightly browned and the cheese is melted.

Sheet Pan French Toast

Servings: 2
Cooking Time: 15 Minutes

Ingredients:
- Oil spray (hand-pumped)
- 2 large eggs
- ¼ cup milk
- 1 teaspoon vanilla extract
- ¼ teaspoon ground cinnamon
- 4 slices whole-grain bread
- ¾ cup maple syrup, or to taste

Directions:
1. Preheat the toaster oven on BAKE to 350°F for 5 minutes.
2. Line the baking tray with parchment paper and generously spray the paper with oil.
3. In a medium bowl, whisk the eggs, milk, vanilla, and cinnamon until well blended.
4. Dredge a slice of bread in the egg mixture until submerged, turn, and take it out. Gently shake the bread to remove any excess egg mixture and place the bread on the baking sheet. Repeat with the remaining bread.
5. Bake for 10 minutes.
6. Flip the bread and bake for 5 minutes longer until both sides are golden brown and crispy.
7. Serve with maple syrup.

New York–style Crumb Cake

Servings: 8

Cooking Time: 90 Minutes

Ingredients:

- CRUMB TOPPING
- 8 tablespoons unsalted butter, melted
- ⅓ cup (2⅓ ounces) granulated sugar
- ⅓ cup packed (2⅓ ounces) dark brown sugar
- ¾ teaspoon ground cinnamon
- ⅛ teaspoon table salt
- 1¾ cups (7 ounces) cake flour
- CAKE
- 1¼ cups (5 ounces) cake flour
- ½ cup (3½ ounces) granulated sugar
- ¼ teaspoon baking soda
- ¼ teaspoon table salt
- 6 tablespoons unsalted butter, cut into 6 pieces and softened
- ⅓ cup buttermilk
- 1 large egg plus 1 large yolk
- 1 teaspoon vanilla extract
- Confectioners' sugar

Directions:

1. Adjust toaster oven rack to middle position and preheat the toaster oven to 325 degrees. Make foil sling for 8-inch square baking pan by folding 2 long sheets of aluminum foil so each is 8 inches wide. Lay sheets of foil in pan perpen-dicular to each other, with extra foil hanging over edges of pan. Push foil into corners and up sides of pan, smoothing foil flush to pan.

2. FOR THE CRUMB TOPPING: Whisk melted butter, granulated sugar, brown sugar, cinnamon, and salt in medium bowl until combined. Add flour and stir with rubber spatula or wooden spoon until mixture resembles thick, cohesive dough; set aside to cool to room temperature, 10 to 15 minutes.

3. FOR THE CAKE: Using stand mixer fitted with paddle, mix flour, sugar, baking soda, and salt on low speed to combine. With mixer running, add softened butter 1 piece at a time. Continue beating until mixture resembles moist crumbs with no visible butter pieces remaining, 1 to 2 minutes. Add buttermilk, egg and yolk, and vanilla and beat on medium-high speed until light and fluffy, about 1 minute, scraping down bowl as needed.

4. Transfer batter to prepared pan. Using rubber spatula, spread batter into even layer. Break apart crumb topping into large pea-size pieces and sprinkle in even layer over batter, beginning with edges and then working toward center. (Assembled cake can be wrapped tightly with plastic wrap and refrigerated for up to 24 hours; increase baking time to 40 to 45 minutes.)

5. Bake until crumbs are golden and toothpick inserted in center of cake comes out clean, 35 to 40 minutes, rotating pan halfway through baking. Let cool on wire rack for at least 30 minutes. Using foil overhang, lift cake out of pan. Dust with confectioners' sugar before serving.

Rosemary Bread

Servings: 6
Cooking Time: 15 Minutes

Ingredients:
- Spread:
- 3 tablespoons olive oil
- 2 tablespoons margarine
- 1 teaspoon garlic
- 2 tablespoons grated Parmesan cheese
- 3 1 tablespoon finely chopped fresh rosemary leaves
- ½ teaspoon freshly ground black pepper
- Salt to taste
- 1 French baguette, sliced 2 inches thick

Directions:
1. Preheat the toaster oven to 350° F.
2. Combine the spread ingredients in a small bowl, blending well with a fork. Adjust the seasonings to taste.
3. Spread the mixture on both sides of the bread slices and wrap the loaf in aluminum foil.
4. BAKE for 10 minutes. Remove from the oven and peel back the foil, exposing the top of the bread loaf. Bake for another 5 minutes, or until the top is lightly browned.

Breakfast Pizza

Servings: 2

Cooking Time: 60 Minutes

Ingredients:

- 3 tablespoons extra-virgin olive oil, divided, plus extra for drizzling
- 1 recipe Classic Pizza Dough (recipe follows), room temperature
- 4 ounces whole-milk mozzarella cheese, shredded (1 cup)
- ½ ounce Parmesan cheese, grated (¼ cup)
- 2 ounces (¼ cup) cottage cheese
- ⅛ teaspoon dried oregano
- 4 ounces breakfast sausage, casings removed
- 4 large eggs
- ⅛ teaspoon table salt
- ⅛ teaspoon pepper
- 2 tablespoons minced fresh chive

Directions:

1. Coat small rimmed baking sheet with 2 tablespoons oil. Press and roll dough into 11 by 8-inch rectangle on lightly floured counter. (If dough springs back during rolling, let rest for 10 minutes before rolling again.) Transfer dough to prepared sheet and re-stretch dough into 11 by 8-inch rectangle. Brush dough evenly with 1 teaspoon oil and cover with plastic wrap. Let sit in warm spot until slightly risen, about 20 minutes.

2. Adjust toaster oven rack to lowest position and preheat the toaster oven to 450 degrees. Remove plastic and, using your fingers, make indentations all over dough. Bake until dough has puffed slightly, 5 to 7 minutes.

3. Combine mozzarella and Parmesan in bowl. Combine cottage cheese, oregano, and remaining 2 teaspoons oil in separate bowl.

4. Remove sheet from oven and, using spatula, press down on any air bubbles. Spread cottage cheese mixture evenly over top, leaving ½-inch border around edges. Pinch sausage into dime-size pieces and arrange evenly over cottage cheese mixture. Sprinkle mozzarella mixture evenly over pizza, leaving ½-inch border. Using back of spoon, create 4 evenly spaced indentations in cheese, each about 3 inches in diameter. Crack 1 egg into each well, then sprinkle with salt and pepper.

5. Bake until crust is golden brown on bottom and eggs are just set, 9 to 10 minutes for slightly runny yolks or 11 to 12 minutes for soft but set yolks. Remove pizza from pan and transfer to wire rack; let rest for 5 minutes. Sprinkle with chives and drizzle with extra oil. Cut into 8 equal pieces and serve.

Nacho Chips

Servings: 12
Cooking Time: 20 Minutes

Ingredients:
- 3 jalapeño peppers
- 4 6-inch flour tortillas
- 1 cup shredded low-fat Cheddar cheese

Directions:
1. Seed and cut the jalapeño peppers into thin rings. Arrange one-fourth of the rings on the tortilla. It's a good idea to wear gloves, since the peppers can sometimes cause skin irritation.
2. Place the tortilla in an oiled or nonstick 8½ × 8½ × 2-inch square baking (cake) pan. Sprinkle evenly with ¼ cup cheese.
3. BROIL for 5 minutes, or until the cheese is melted. Repeat the process for the remaining tortillas. Cut each into 6 wedges with a sharp knife or scissors.

Bacon, Broccoli And Swiss Cheese Bread Pudding

Servings: 2
Cooking Time: 48 Minutes

Ingredients:
- ½ pound thick cut bacon, cut into ¼-inch pieces
- 3 cups brioche bread or rolls, cut into ½-inch cubes
- 3 eggs
- 1 cup milk
- ½ teaspoon salt
- freshly ground black pepper
- 1 cup frozen broccoli florets, thawed and chopped
- 1½ cups grated Swiss cheese

Directions:
1. Preheat the toaster oven to 400°F.
2. Air-fry the bacon for 6 minutes until crispy, rotate a few times while it cooks to help it cook evenly. Remove the bacon and set it aside on a paper towel.
3. Air-fry the brioche bread cubes for 2 minutes to dry and toast lightly. (If your brioche is a few days old and slightly stale, you can omit this step.)
4. Butter a 6- or 7-inch cake pan. Combine all the ingredients in a large bowl and toss well. Transfer the mixture to the buttered cake pan, cover with aluminum foil and refrigerate the bread pudding overnight, or for at least 8 hours.
5. Remove the casserole from the refrigerator an hour before you plan to cook, and let it sit on the countertop to come to room temperature.
6. Preheat the toaster oven to 330°F. Transfer the covered cake pan, to the air fryer oven, lowering the dish into the air fryer oven using a sling made of aluminum foil (fold a piece of aluminum foil into a strip about 2-inches wide by 24-inches long). Fold the ends of the aluminum foil over the top of the dish before returning to the air fryer oven. Air-fry for 20 minutes. Remove the foil and air-fry for an additional 20 minutes. If the top starts to brown a little too much before the custard has set, simply return the foil to the pan. The bread pudding has cooked through when a skewer inserted into the center comes out clean.

Mini Pita Breads

Servings: 8

Cooking Time: 6 Minutes

Ingredients:

- 2 teaspoons active dry yeast
- 1 tablespoon sugar
- 1¼ to 1½ cups warm water (90° - 110°F)
- 3¼ cups all-purpose flour
- 2 teaspoons salt
- 1 tablespoon olive oil, plus more for brushing
- kosher salt (optional)

Directions:

1. Dissolve the yeast, sugar and water in the bowl of a stand mixer. Let the mixture sit for 5 minutes to make sure the yeast is active – it should foam a little. (If there's no foaming, discard and start again with new yeast.) Combine the flour and salt in a bowl, and add it to the water, along with the olive oil. Mix with the dough hook until combined. Add a little more flour if needed to get the dough to pull away from the sides of the mixing bowl, or add a little more water if the dough seems too dry.

2. Knead the dough until it is smooth and elastic (about 8 minutes in the mixer or 15 minutes by hand). Transfer the dough to a lightly oiled bowl, cover and let it rise in a warm place until doubled in bulk. Divide the dough into 8 portions and roll each portion into a circle about 4-inches in diameter. Don't roll the balls too thin, or you won't get the pocket inside the pita.

3. Preheat the toaster oven to 400°F.

4. Brush both sides of the dough with olive oil, and sprinkle with kosher salt if desired. Air-fry one at a time at 400°F for 6 minutes, flipping it over when there are two minutes left in the cooking time.

Mushroom Blue Cheese Crostini

Servings: 10

Cooking Time: 3 Minutes

Ingredients:

- 1 tablespoon olive oil
- 8 ounces mushrooms, wild or button, sliced
- 3 cloves garlic, minced
- 2 tablespoons fresh flat-leaf (Italian) parsley, minced
- 2 teaspoons chopped fresh thyme, rosemary, or sage leaves
- Kosher salt and freshly ground black pepper
- 10 to 12 country bread, artisan bread, or baguette slices
- 1 cup grated fontina cheese
- ½ cup blue cheese or Gorgonzola crumbles
- 1 tablespoon fresh lemon juice
- Whole flat-leaf (Italian) parsley, for garnish

Directions:

1. Heat the olive oil in a medium nonstick skillet over medium-high heat. Add the mushrooms and cook, stirring frequently, until the liquid has evaporated, 7 to 10 minutes. Add the garlic and cook for 1 minute. Remove from the heat. Stir in the parsley and thyme and season with salt and pepper. Allow the mixture to cool.
2. Toast the slices of bread in the toaster oven.
3. Stir the fontina and blue cheese into the mushroom mixture.
4. Preheat the toaster oven on 400°F. Arrange the toasted baguette slices on a 12 x 12-inch baking sheet. Distribute the mushroom cheese mixture evenly over the toasted bread slices. Broil until the cheese melts, 2 to 3 minutes. Drizzle with the lemon juice. Garnish each crostini with a parsley leaf. Serve immediately.

Brown Sugar Grapefruit

Servings: 2
Cooking Time: 4 Minutes

Ingredients:

- 1 grapefruit
- 2 to 4 teaspoons brown sugar

Directions:

1. Preheat the toaster oven to 400°F.
2. While the air fryer oven is Preheating, cut the grapefruit in half horizontally (in other words not through the stem or blossom end of the grapefruit). Slice the bottom of the grapefruit to help it sit flat on the counter if necessary. Using a sharp paring knife (serrated is great), cut around the grapefruit between the flesh of the fruit and the peel. Then, cut each segment away from the membrane so that it is sitting freely in the fruit.
3. Sprinkle 1 to 2 teaspoons of brown sugar on each half of the prepared grapefruit. Set up a rack in the air fryer oven (use an air fryer oven rack or make your own rack with some crumpled up aluminum foil). You don't have to use a rack, but doing so will get the grapefruit closer to the element so that the brown sugar can caramelize a little better. Transfer the grapefruit half to the rack in the air fryer oven. Depending on how big your grapefruit are and what size air fryer oven you have, you may need to do each half separately to make sure they sit flat.
4. Air-fry at 400°F for 4 minutes.
5. Remove and let it cool for just a minute before enjoying.

Yogurt Bread

Servings: 2
Cooking Time: 40 Minutes

Ingredients:

- 3 cups unbleached flour
- 4 teaspoons baking powder
- 5 2 teaspoons sugar
- Salt to taste
- 1 cup plain nonfat yogurt
- ¼ cup vegetable oil
- 1 egg, beaten, to brush the top

Directions:

1. Preheat the toaster oven to 375° F.
2. Combine the flour, baking powder, sugar, and salt in a large bowl. Make a hole in the center and spoon in the yogurt and oil.
3. Stir the flour into the center. When the dough is well mixed, turn it out onto a lightly floured surface and knead for 8 minutes, until the dough is smooth and elastic. Place the dough in an oiled or nonstick regular-size 8½ × 4½ × 2¼-inch loaf pan. Brush the top with the beaten egg.
4. BAKE for 40 minutes, or until a toothpick inserted in the center comes out clean and the loaf is browned. Invert on a wire rack to cool.

Creamy Bacon + Almond Crostini

Servings: 20

Cooking Time: 10 Minutes

Ingredients:

- 1 baguette loaf, cut into ½-inch-thick slices
- 2 tablespoons olive oil
- 4 ounces cream cheese, cut into cubes, softened
- ½ cup mayonnaise
- 1 cup shredded fontina cheese or Monterey Jack cheese
- 4 slices bacon, cooked until crisp and crumbled
- 1 green onion, white and green portions, finely chopped
- ¼ teaspoon Sriracha or hot sauce
- Dash kosher salt
- ¼ cup sliced almonds, toasted
- Minced fresh flat-leaf (Italian) parsley

Directions:

1. Toast the slices of the baguette in the toaster oven.
2. Arrange the toasted baguette slices on a 12-inch pizza pan or a 12 x 12-inch baking pan. Lightly brush the slices with the olive oil.
3. Preheat the toaster oven to 375°F.
4. Beat the cream cheese and mayonnaise in a medium bowl with an electric mixer at medium speed until creamy and smooth. Stir in the fontina, bacon, green onion, Sriracha, and salt and blend until combined.
5. Distribute the cheese mixture evenly over the toasted bread. Top with the sliced almonds. Bake for 6 to 8 minutes or until the cheese is hot and beginning to melt. Allow to cool for 1 to 2 minutes, then garnish with minced parsley. Serve warm.

LUNCH AND DINNER

Salad Couscous

Servings: 4

Cooking Time: 10 Minutes

Ingredients:

- 1 10-ounce package precooked couscous
- 2 tablespoons olive oil
- Salt and freshly ground black pepper
- ¼ cup chopped fresh tomatoes
- 2 tablespoons chopped fresh basil leaves
- 1 tablespoon sliced almonds
- ½ bell pepper, chopped
- 3 scallions, chopped
- 2 tablespoons lemon juice

Directions:

1. Preheat the toaster oven to 400° F.

2. Mix together the couscous, 2 cups water, and olive oil in a 1-quart 8½ × 8½ × 4-inch ovenproof baking dish. Add salt and pepper to taste. Cover with aluminum foil.

3. BAKE, covered, for 10 minutes, or until the couscous is cooked. Remove from the oven, fluff with a fork and, when cool, add the tomatoes, basil leaves, almonds, pepper, scallions, and lemon juice. Adjust the seasonings to taste. Chill before serving.

Chicken Gumbo

Servings: 4

Cooking Time: 40 Minutes

Ingredients:

- 2 skinless, boneless chicken breast halves, cut into 1-inch cubes
- ½ cup dry red wine
- 1 small onion, finely chopped
- 1 celery stalk, finely chopped
- 2 plum tomatoes, chopped
- 3 1 bell pepper, chopped
- 1 tablespoon minced fresh garlic
- 2 okra pods, stemmed, seeded, and finely chopped 1 bay leaf
- ½ teaspoon hot sauce
- ½ teaspoon dried thyme
- Salt and freshly ground black pepper to taste

Directions:

1. Preheat the toaster oven to 400° F.

2. Combine all the ingredients in a 1-quart 8½ × 8½ × 4-inch ovenproof baking dish. Adjust the seasonings to taste. Cover with aluminum foil.

3. BAKE, covered, for 40 minutes, or until the onion, pepper, and celery are tender. Discard the bay leaf before serving.

Herbal Summer Casserole

Servings: 4
Cooking Time: 45 Minutes

Ingredients:

- 4 small yellow (summer) squashes, cut into ¾-inch slices
- 1 green bell pepper, seeded and chopped
- 1 tablespoon roasted garlic, mashed in 1 tablespoon olive oil
- ¼ cup seasoned bread crumbs
- ¼ cup grated Parmesan cheese
- ¼ cup chopped fresh parsley
- 2 tablespoons chopped fresh cilantro
- 2 tablespoons chopped onion
- 2 plum tomatoes, chopped
- 2 carrots, peeled and cut into ¼-inch slices
- 4 tablespoons fresh lemon juice
- ½ teaspoon caraway seeds
- ¼ teaspoon celery seed
- Salt and freshly ground black pepper to taste

Directions:

1. Preheat the toaster oven to 400° F.
2. Combine all the ingredients in a 1-quart 8½ × 8½ × 4-inch ovenproof baking dish, mixing well. Cover the dish with aluminum foil.
3. BAKE, covered, for 45 minutes, or until the vegetables are tender.

Maple Bacon

Servings: 6
Cooking Time: 16 Minutes

Ingredients:

- 12 slices bacon
- ½ cup packed dark brown sugar
- 2 tablespoons maple syrup
- 1 teaspoon Dijon mustard
- 2 tablespoons red or white wine

Directions:

1. Preheat the toaster oven to 350°F. Line a 12 x 12-inch baking pan with aluminum foil.
2. Place 6 bacon strips on the prepared pan, leaving space between the strips. Bake for 10 minutes or until the bacon is almost crisp. Carefully drain the bacon and return it to the pan.
3. Combine the brown sugar, maple syrup, mustard, and wine in a small bowl. Blend until smooth. Brush the glaze over the bacon. Bake for 8 minutes. Turn the bacon and brush with the glaze. Continue to bake for an additional 6 to 8 minutes, or until golden brown.
4. Repeat with the remaining bacon strips.

Tarragon Beef Ragout

Ingredients:

- 1 pound lean round steak, cut across the grain of the meat into thin strips, approximately ¼ × 2 inches
- ½ cup dry red wine
- 1 small onion, chopped
- 2 carrots, peeled and thinly sliced
- 3 2 plum tomatoes, chopped
- 1 celery stalk, chopped
- 1 10-ounce package frozen peas
- 3 garlic gloves, minced
- 1 tablespoon Dijon mustard
- ½ teaspoon ground cumin
- ½ teaspoon dried tarragon
- Salt and freshly ground black pepper to taste

Directions:

1. Preheat the toaster oven to 375° F.
2. Combine all the ingredients with ½ cup water in an 8½ × 8½ × 4-inch ovenproof baking dish. Adjust the seasonings. Cover with aluminum foil.
3. BAKE, covered, for 45 minutes, or until the beef, onion, and celery are tender. Remove the cover.
4. BROIL 8 minutes to reduce the liquid and lightly brown the top.

Couscous-stuffed Poblano Peppers

Servings: 6

Cooking Time: 35 Minutes

Ingredients:

- 2 tablespoons olive oil
- ⅔ cup Israeli couscous
- 1 ¼ cups vegetable broth or water
- Kosher salt and freshly ground black pepper
- ½ medium onion, chopped
- 2 cloves garlic, minced
- 1 teaspoon dried oregano leaves
- ½ teaspoon ground cumin
- 1 (14.5-ounce) can fire-roasted diced tomatoes, with liquid
- Nonstick cooking spray
- 3 large poblano peppers, halved lengthwise, seeds and stem removed
- 1 ½ cups shredded Mexican blend, pepper Jack, or sharp cheddar cheese
- Optional toppings: minced fresh cilantro, sliced jalapeño peppers, diced tomatoes, sliced green onions (white and green portions)

Directions:

1. Heat 1 tablespoon oil in a medium saucepan over medium heat. Add the couscous and cook, stirring frequently, until golden brown, 2 to 3 minutes. Stir in the broth and season with salt and pepper. Cover, reduce the heat to a simmer, and cook, stirring occasionally, for about 10 minutes or until the liquid is absorbed. Remove from the heat and let stand, covered, for 5 minutes. Remove the cover, stir, and set aside to cool.

2. Heat the remaining 1 tablespoon oil in a small saucepan over medium heat. Add the onion, and cook, stirring frequently, for 3 to 5 minutes or until tender. Stir in the garlic and cook for 30 seconds. Stir in the oregano and cumin and season with salt and pepper. Stir in the tomatoes and simmer for 5 minutes.

3. Preheat the toaster oven to 400°F. Spray a 9-inch square baking pan with nonstick cooking spray. Spoon about one-third of the tomato mixture into the prepared pan. Arrange the peppers, cut side up, in the pan.

4. Stir 1 cup of the cheese into the couscous. Spoon the couscous mixture into the peppers, mounding slightly. Spoon the remaining tomato mixture over the peppers. Cover the pan and bake for 30 minutes.

5. Uncover the pan and sprinkle with the remaining cheese. Bake for 5 minutes or until the cheese is melted.

6. Top as desired with any of the various topping choices.

Quick Pan Pizza

Servings: 8

Cooking Time: 22 Minutes

Ingredients:

- 1 can (13.8 oz.) refrigerator pizza crust, cut in half
- 2 tablespoons oil, divided
- 2/3 cup Slow Cooker Marinara Sauce, divided
- 2 cups shredded mozzarella cheese, divided
- 18 slices pepperoni, divided
- 1 small green pepper, sliced into rings, divided
- 2 large mushrooms, sliced, divided

Directions:

1. Preheat the toaster oven to 425°F. Spray baking pan with nonstick cooking spray.
2. Press half of dough into pan. Brush with 1 tablespoon oil.
3. Bake 8 to 9 minutes or until light brown.
4. Top baked crust with 1/3 cup sauce, 1 cup shredded mozzarella cheese and half of the pepperoni, green pepper and mushrooms.
5. Bake an additional 11 to 13 minutes or until cheese is melted and crust is brown. Repeat to make second pizza.

Cheesy Chicken–stuffed Shells

Servings: 4

Cooking Time: 40 Minutes

Ingredients:

- Nonstick cooking spray
- 16 jumbo pasta shells
- 1 cup finely diced cooked chicken
- 1 cup whole milk ricotta cheese
- 1 ¼ cups shredded mozzarella cheese
- 1 large egg, slightly beaten
- ⅓ cup grated Parmesan cheese
- 1 teaspoon Italian seasoning
- 2 cloves garlic, minced
- ¼ teaspoon kosher salt
- ¼ teaspoon freshly ground black pepper
- 1 ½ cups marinara sauce

Directions:

1. Preheat the toaster oven to 350 °F. Spray an 8 x 8-inch square baking pan with nonstick cooking spray.
2. Cook the shells according to the package directions, drain, and rinse with cool water.
3. Combine the chicken, ricotta, ¾ cup of the mozzarella, egg, Parmesan, Italian seasoning, garlic, salt, and pepper in a large bowl.
4. Spread about ¾ cup of the marinara sauce in the prepared pan. Fill each shell with a heaping tablespoon of the chicken-cheese mixture. Place the prepared shells, stuffed side up, in the pan. Pour the remaining marinara over the shells.
5. Cover and bake for 25 to 30 minutes. Sprinkle with the remaining ½ cup mozzarella and bake, uncovered, for an additional 5 to 10 minutes or until the cheese is melted. Remove from the oven and let stand for 5 to 10 minutes before serving.

Chicken Thighs With Roasted Rosemary Root Vegetables

Servings: 2

Cooking Time: 70 Minutes

Ingredients:

- 2 sprigs fresh rosemary
- 1 small turnip, peeled and cut into 1 1/2-inch cubes
- 1 parsnip, peeled and cut into 1/2-inch slices
- 1 small onion, quartered
- 1 large sweet potato, peeled and cut into 1-inch cubes
- 2 cloves garlic, peeled
- 2 tablespoons olive oil
- 1 teaspoon salt, divided
- 1/2 teaspoon coarse pepper, divided
- 1/2 teaspoon rotisserie chicken seasoning
- 4 chicken thighs with bone and skin

Directions:

1. Place rack on bottom position of toaster oven. Preheat the toaster oven to 425°F.
2. Spray the toaster oven baking pan with nonstick cooking spray. Place rosemary sprigs on pan.
3. In a large bowl, mix turnip. parsnip, onion, sweet potato, garlic, oil, 1/2 teaspoon salt and 1/4 teaspoon pepper until vegetables are coated with oil. Add to baking pan.
4. Bake 30 minutes. Stir vegetables.
5. Sprinkle remaining salt, pepper and rotisserie chicken seasoning over chicken pieces.
6. Place chicken on top of vegetables in pan. Continue baking for an additional 35 to 40 minutes or until chicken reaches 165°F when tested with a meat thermometer and vegetables are roasted.

Roasted Harissa Chicken + Vegetables

Servings: 4

Cooking Time: 30 Minutes

Ingredients:

- Nonstick cooking spray
- 1 medium zucchini, halved lengthwise and sliced crosswise ½ inch thick
- ½ large red onion, sliced ¼ inch thick
- 2 tablespoons olive oil
- Kosher salt and freshly ground black pepper
- 1 pound boneless, skinless chicken breasts, cut into 1-inch cubes
- ½ teaspoon ground cumin
- 1 clove garlic, minced
- 2 tablespoons harissa sauce or paste
- 1 tablespoon honey
- 2 tablespoons minced fresh cilantro
- 2 cups hot cooked rice
- Optional toppings: plain Greek yogurt or sour cream, sesame seeds (toasted or chopped), or dry-roasted peanuts

Directions:

1. Preheat the toaster oven to 400°F. Spray a 12 x 12-inch baking pan with nonstick cooking spray.

2. Place the zucchini and red onion in a medium bowl. Drizzle with 1 tablespoon olive oil and season with salt and pepper. Stir to coat the vegetables evenly. Arrange the vegetables in a single layer in the prepared baking pan. Roast, uncovered, for 10 minutes.

3. Place the chicken cubes in that same bowl. Drizzle with the remaining 1 tablespoon olive oil. Season with the cumin, garlic, salt, and pepper. Stir to coat the chicken evenly.

4. Stir the vegetables and move to one side of the pan. Arrange the chicken in a single layer on the other side of the pan. Roast for 10 minutes.

5. Blend the harissa and honey in a small bowl. Drizzle the sauce over the chicken and vegetables. Using a pastry brush, coat the chicken and vegetables evenly. Roast, uncovered, for an additional 8 to 10 minutes, or until the vegetables are tender and the chicken registers 165°F on a meat thermometer.

6. Spoon the chicken, vegetables, and any collected liquid onto a serving platter. Sprinkle with the cilantro. Serve the chicken and vegetables with the rice and, if desired, a dollop of plain Greek yogurt and a sprinkling of sesame seeds.

Fresh Herb Veggie Pizza

Servings: 4

Cooking Time: 25 Minutes

Ingredients:

- 1 9-inch ready-made pizza crust
- 1 tablespoon olive oil
- 1 4-ounce can tomato paste
- 2 tablespoons shredded part-skim mozzarella
- 2 tablespoons grated Parmesan cheese
- 2 tablespoons crumbled feta cheese
- ½ bell pepper, chopped
- 1 tablespoon chopped fresh parsley
- 1 tablespoon chopped fresh oregano
- 1 tablespoon chopped fresh basil
- ½ teaspoon red pepper flakes
- Salt and freshly ground black pepper to taste
- Pizza mixture:
- 2 garlic cloves, minced
- 1 plum tomato, chopped

Directions:

1. Preheat the toaster oven to 400° F.
2. Brush the pizza crust with olive oil and spread the tomato paste evenly to cover.
3. Combine the ingredients for the pizza mixture and spread evenly on top of the tomato paste layer. Sprinkle the cheeses over all and season to taste. Place the pizza on the toaster oven rack.
4. BAKE for 25 minutes, or until the vegetables are cooked and the cheese is melted.

Middle Eastern Roasted Chicken

Servings: 4

Cooking Time: 25 Minutes

Ingredients:

- 3 tablespoons fresh lemon juice
- ¼ cup plus 1 tablespoon olive oil
- 4 cloves garlic, minced
- ½ teaspoon kosher salt
- 1 teaspoon freshly ground black pepper
- 1 teaspoon ground cumin
- 1 teaspoon paprika
- ½ teaspoon turmeric
- ⅛ teaspoon red pepper flakes
- 1 pound boneless, skinless chicken breasts
- 1 large onion, cut into thin wedges

Directions:

1. Whisk the lemon juice, ¼ cup olive oil, garlic, salt, pepper, cumin, paprika, turmeric, and red pepper flakes in a small bowl until blended.

2. Cut the chicken breast lengthwise into thin scaloppine slices. Place the chicken in a nonreactive dish and pour the marinade over the chicken. Turn the chicken to coat thoroughly and evenly. Cover, refrigerate, and marinate for at least 1 hour and up to 10 hours. (The longer the better, as the flavor melds with the chicken.)

3. Remove the chicken from the refrigerator and add the onion to the marinade.

4. Preheat the toaster oven to 425°F. Brush the remaining tablespoon of olive oil over the bottom of a 12 x 12-inch pan. Place the chicken pieces on one side of the baking sheet and the onion wedges on the other side in a single layer. Discard any remaining marinade.

5. Roast for 20 to 25 minutes or until the chicken is browned and a meat thermometer registers 165°F. Remove from the oven and let rest a few minutes, then slice the chicken into thin strips. Toss with the onion and serve.

Nice + Easy Baked Macaroni + Cheese

Servings: 6

Cooking Time: 35 Minutes

Ingredients:

- Nonstick cooking spray
- 2 cups whole milk
- 3 ounces cream cheese
- ½ teaspoon kosher salt
- 1 clove garlic
- ¼ teaspoon freshly ground black pepper
- 8 ounces macaroni, uncooked
- 2 cups shredded cheddar cheese
- 2 tablespoons unsalted butter, melted
- ¼ cup grated Parmesan cheese
- 1 cup panko bread crumbs

Directions:

1. Preheat the toaster oven to 425°F. Spray an 11 x 7 x 2 ½-inch baking dish with nonstick cooking spray.
2. Place the milk, cream cheese, salt, garlic, and pepper into a blender. Blend until smooth.
3. Add macaroni to the prepared dish. Sprinkle with the cheddar cheese. Pour the milk mixture over all.
4. Combine the butter, Parmesan, and panko in a small bowl. Sprinkle the crumb mixture over the macaroni. Bake, uncovered, for 25 to 35 minutes or until the top is golden brown. Remove from the oven and let stand for at least 10 minutes.

Individual Chicken Pot Pies

Servings: 4
Cooking Time: 25 Minutes

Ingredients:

- 3 tablespoons unsalted butter
- ½ medium onion, chopped
- 1 carrot, chopped
- 1 stalk celery, chopped
- 1 ¼ cups sliced button or white mushrooms
- 2 tablespoons all-purpose flour
- 1 ¼ cups whole milk
- 1 tablespoon fresh lemon juice
- ½ teaspoon dried thyme leaves
- Kosher salt and freshly ground black pepper
- 1 ½ cups chopped cooked chicken
- ½ cup frozen peas
- Nonstick cooking spray
- 1 sheet frozen puff pastry, about 9 inches square, thawed (½ of a 17.3-ounce package)
- 1 large egg

Directions:

1. Melt the butter in a large skillet over medium-high heat. Add the onion, carrot, and celery and cook, stirring frequently, for 3 minutes. Add the mushrooms and cook, stirring frequently, for 7 to 10 minutes or until the liquid has evaporated. Blend in the flour and cook, stirring for 1 minute. (Be sure all of the flour is blended into the butter and vegetables.) Gradually stir in the milk. Cook, stirring constantly, until the mixture bubbles and thickens. Stir in the lemon juice and thyme and season with salt and pepper. Stir in the chicken and peas. Remove from the heat and set aside.

2. Preheat the toaster oven to 375°F. Spray 4 (8-ounce) oven-safe ramekins with nonstick cooking spray.

3. Roll the puff pastry out on a lightly floured board, to make an even 10-inch square. Cut the pastry into circles using a 4-inch cutter.

4. Spoon a heaping ¾ cup of filling into each prepared ramekin. Place a puff pastry circle on top of each and crimp the edges to seal to the ramekin. Using the tip of a paring knife, cut 3 slits in each crust to allow steam to escape. Whisk the egg with 1 tablespoon water in a small bowl. Brush the egg mixture over the top of the crust.

5. Bake for 20 to 25 minutes, or until the crust is golden brown. Remove from the oven and let stand for 5 minutes before serving.

Honey Bourbon–glazed Pork Chops With Sweet Potatoes + Apples

Servings: 2

Cooking Time: 42 Minutes

Ingredients:

- Nonstick cooking spray
- 2 medium sweet potatoes, peeled and quartered
- 2 tablespoons bourbon
- 2 tablespoons honey
- 1 tablespoon canola or vegetable oil
- ½ teaspoon onion powder
- ½ teaspoon dry mustard
- ¼ teaspoon dried thyme leaves
- Kosher salt and freshly ground black pepper
- 2 bone-in pork chops, cut about ¾ inch thick
- 1 Granny Smith apple, not peeled, cored and cut into ½-inch wedges

Directions:

1. Preheat the toaster oven to 375°F. Spray a 12 x 12-inch baking pan with nonstick cooking spray.

2. Place the sweet potatoes on one side of the prepared pan. Spray with nonstick cooking spray. Bake, uncovered, for 20 minutes.

3. Meanwhile, stir the bourbon, honey, oil, onion powder, mustard, and thyme in a small bowl. Season with salt and pepper and set aside.

4. Turn the potatoes over. Place the pork chops on the other end of the pan in a single layer. Arrange the apple wedges around the potatoes and pork chops, stacking the apples as needed. Brush the bourbon mixture generously over all. Bake for 15 to 18 minutes or until the pork is done as desired and a meat thermometer registers a minimum of 145°F.

5. For additional browning, set the toaster oven to Broil and broil for 2 to 4 minutes, or until the edges are brown as desired.

6. Transfer to a serving platter. Spoon any drippings over the meat and vegetables. Let stand for 5 minutes before serving.

Scalloped Corn Casserole

Servings: 4

Cooking Time: 38 Minutes

Ingredients:

- Casserole mixture:
- 2 15-ounce cans corn
- 1 red bell pepper, chopped
- ¼ cup chopped scallions
- ½ cup fat-free half-and-half
- 2 tablespoons unbleached flour
- 2 eggs
- ½ teaspoon chili powder
- 1 teaspoon ground cumin
- 1 teaspoon garlic powder
- Salt and freshly ground black pepper to taste
- ¼ cup multigrain seasoned bread Crumbs
- 1 tablespoon margarine

Directions:

1. Preheat the toaster oven to 400° F.

2. Combine all the casserole mixture ingredients in a 1-quart 8½ × 8½ × 4-inch ovenproof baking dish, mixing well. Adjust the seasonings to taste. Cover with aluminum foil.

3. BAKE, covered, for 30 minutes, or until the pepper and onions are tender. Remove from the oven and uncover. Sprinkle with the bread crumbs and dot with the margarine.

4. BROIL for 8 minutes, or until the bread crumb topping is lightly browned.

Healthy Southwest Stuffed Peppers

Servings: 6
Cooking Time: 30 Minutes

Ingredients:

- 1 tablespoon oil
- 1 small onion, chopped
- 1 garlic clove, minced
- 1/2 pound ground turkey
- 1/2 cup drained black beans
- 1/2 cup whole kernel corn
- 1 jar (16 oz.) medium salsa, divided
- 1/2 cup cooked white rice
- 1/2 teaspoon chili powder
- 1/2 teaspoon salt
- 1/4 teaspoon ground cumin
- 1/4 teaspoon black pepper
- 3 medium peppers, halved lengthwise leaving stem on, seeded
- 1/3 cup shredded Monterey Jack cheese, divided
- Sour cream
- Chopped fresh cilantro

Directions:

1. Preheat the toaster oven to 350°F. Spray baking pan with nonstick cooking spray.
2. In a large skillet over medium-high, heat oil. Add onion and garlic, cook for 2 to 3 minutes.
3. Add turkey to skillet, cook, stirring frequently, for 6 to 8 minutes or until turkey is cooked through.
4. Stir black beans, corn, 1/2 cup salsa, rice, chili powder, salt, cumin and pepper into turkey mixture.
5. Fill each pepper half with turkey mixture, dividing mixture evenly among peppers.
6. Top each pepper half with remaining salsa.
7. Bake 20 minutes. Sprinkle with cheese and bake an additional 10 minutes or until heated through.
8. Top with sour cream and cilantro.

Gardener's Rice

Servings: 4

Cooking Time: 40 Minutes

Ingredients:

- ½ cup rice
- 2 tablespoons finely chopped scallions
- 2 small zucchini, finely chopped
- 1 bell pepper, finely chopped
- 1 small tomato, finely chopped
- ¼ cup frozen peas
- ¼ cup frozen corn
- 1 teaspoon ground cumin
- ½ teaspoon dried oregano or
- 1 teaspoon chopped fresh oregano
- Salt and freshly ground black pepper to taste

Directions:

1. Preheat the toaster oven to 400° F.

2. Combine all the ingredients with ¼ cups water in a 1-quart 8½ × 8½ × 4-inch ovenproof baking dish, stirring well to blend. Adjust the seasonings to taste. Cover with aluminum foil.

3. BAKE, covered, for 30 minutes, or until the rice and vegetables are almost cooked. Remove from the oven, uncover, and let stand for 10 minutes to complete the cooking. Fluff once more and adjust the seasonings before serving.

Spicy Oven-baked Chili

Servings: 6

Cooking Time: 30 Minutes

Ingredients:

- 1 pound lean ground turkey or ground chicken breast or 1 pound lean ground sirloin or round steak
- 1 15-ounce can black beans, drained
- 1 8-ounce can tomato sauce
- ¾ cup chopped onion
- ¼ cup dry white wine
- 1 cup tomato salsa
- 1 tablespoon garlic powder
- 1 tablespoon chili powder
- 2 ⅛ teaspoon cayenne
- 3 teaspoons unsweetened cocoa
- Salt and butcher's pepper to taste

Directions:

1. Preheat the toaster oven to 375° F.

2. Combine all the ingredients in a 1-quart 8½ × 8½ × 4-inch ovenproof baking dish and mix well. Adjust the seasonings to taste. Cover with aluminum foil.

3. BAKE, covered, for 30 minutes.

FISH AND SEAFOOD

Fish With Sun-dried Tomato Pesto

Servings: 4
Cooking Time: 31 Minutes

Ingredients:

- Tomato sauce:
- ¼ cup chopped sun-dried tomatoes
- 2 tablespoons chopped fresh basil
- ⅔ cup dry white wine
- 2 tablespoons grated Parmesan cheese
- 2 tablespoons olive oil
- 1 tablespoon pine nuts
- 2 garlic cloves
- Salt and freshly ground black pepper to taste
- 4 6-ounce fish fillets (trout, catfish, flounder, or tilapia)
- 1 tablespoon reduced-fat mayonnaise
- 2 tablespoons chopped fresh cilantro Olive oil

Directions:

1. Preheat the toaster oven to 400° F.
2. Process the tomato sauce ingredients in a blender or food processor until smooth.
3. Layer the fish fillets in an oiled or nonstick 8½ × 8½ × 2-inch square baking (cake) pan. Spoon the sauce over the fish, spreading evenly.
4. BAKE, uncovered, for 25 minutes, or until the fish flakes easily with a fork. Remove from the oven, spread the mayonnaise on top of the fish, and garnish with the cilantro.
5. BROIL for 6 minutes, or until lightly browned.

Stuffed Baked Red Snapper

Servings: 2
Cooking Time: 30 Minutes

Ingredients:

- Stuffing mixture:
- 12 medium shrimp, cooked, peeled, and chopped
- 2 tablespoons multigrain bread crumbs
- 1 teaspoon anchovy paste
- ¼ teaspoon paprika
- Salt to taste
- 2 6-ounce red snapper fillets
- 1 egg
- ½ cup fat-free half-and-half
- 2 tablespoons cooking sherry

Directions:

1. Preheat the toaster oven to 350° F.
2. Combine all the stuffing mixture ingredients in a medium bowl and place a mound of mixture on one end of each fillet. Fold over the other fillet end, skewering the edge with toothpicks.
3. Place the rolled fillets in an oiled or nonstick 8½ × 8½ × 2-inch square baking (cake) pan.
4. Whisk the egg in a small bowl until light in color, then whisk in the half-and-half and sherry. Pour over the fillets. Cover the pan with aluminum foil.
5. BAKE for 30 minutes.

Better Fish Sticks

Servings: 3

Cooking Time: 8 Minutes

Ingredients:

- ¾ cup Seasoned Italian-style dried bread crumbs (gluten-free, if a concern)
- 3 tablespoons (about ½ ounce) Finely grated Parmesan cheese
- 10 ounces Skinless cod fillets, cut lengthwise into 1-inch-wide pieces
- 3 tablespoons Regular or low-fat mayonnaise (not fat-free; gluten-free, if a concern)
- Vegetable oil spray

Directions:

1. Preheat the toaster oven to 400°F.
2. Mix the bread crumbs and grated Parmesan in a shallow soup bowl or a small pie plate.
3. Smear the fish fillet sticks completely with the mayonnaise, then dip them one by one in the bread-crumb mixture, turning and pressing gently to make an even and thorough coating. Coat each stick on all sides with vegetable oil spray.
4. Set the fish sticks in the air fryer oven with at least ¼ inch between them. Air-fry undisturbed for 8 minutes, or until golden brown and crisp.
5. Use a nonstick-safe spatula to gently transfer them from the air fryer oven to a wire rack. Cool for only a minute or two before serving.

Maple Balsamic Glazed Salmon

Servings: 4

Cooking Time: 10 Minutes

Ingredients:

- 4 (6-ounce) fillets of salmon
- salt and freshly ground black pepper
- vegetable oil
- ¼ cup pure maple syrup
- 3 tablespoons balsamic vinegar
- 1 teaspoon Dijon mustard

Directions:

1. Preheat the toaster oven to 400°F.
2. Season the salmon well with salt and freshly ground black pepper. Spray or brush the bottom of the air fryer oven with vegetable oil and place the salmon fillets inside. Air-fry the salmon for 5 minutes.
3. While the salmon is air-frying, combine the maple syrup, balsamic vinegar and Dijon mustard in a small saucepan over medium heat and stir to blend well. Let the mixture simmer while the fish is cooking. It should start to thicken slightly, but keep your eye on it so it doesn't burn.
4. Brush the glaze on the salmon fillets and air-fry for an additional 5 minutes. The salmon should feel firm to the touch when finished and the glaze should be nicely browned on top. Brush a little more glaze on top before removing and serving with rice and vegetables, or a nice green salad.

Fried Shrimp

Servings: 3
Cooking Time: 7 Minutes

Ingredients:

- 1 Large egg white
- 2 tablespoons Water
- 1 cup Plain dried bread crumbs (gluten-free, if a concern)
- ¼ cup All-purpose flour or almond flour
- ¼ cup Yellow cornmeal
- 1 teaspoon Celery salt
- 1 teaspoon Mild paprika
- Up to ½ teaspoon Cayenne (optional)
- ¾ pound Large shrimp (20–25 per pound), peeled and deveined
- Vegetable oil spray

Directions:

1. Preheat the toaster oven to 400°F.
2. Set two medium or large bowls on your counter. In the first, whisk the egg white and water until foamy. In the second, stir the bread crumbs, flour, cornmeal, celery salt, paprika, and cayenne (if using) until well combined.
3. Pour all the shrimp into the egg white mixture and stir gently until all the shrimp are coated. Use kitchen tongs to pick them up one by one and transfer them to the bread-crumb mixture. Turn each in the bread-crumb mixture to coat it evenly and thoroughly on all sides before setting it on a cutting board. When you're done coating the shrimp, coat them all on both sides with the vegetable oil spray.
4. Set the shrimp in as close to one layer in the air fryer oven as you can. Some may overlap. Air-fry for 7 minutes, gently rearranging the shrimp at the 4-minute mark to get covered surfaces exposed, until golden brown and firm but not hard.
5. Use kitchen tongs to gently transfer the shrimp to a wire rack. Cool for only a minute or two before serving.

Bacon-wrapped Scallops

Servings: 4
Cooking Time: 8 Minutes

Ingredients:

- 16 large scallops
- 8 bacon strips
- ½ teaspoon black pepper
- ¼ teaspoon smoked paprika

Directions:

1. Pat the scallops dry with a paper towel. Slice each of the bacon strips in half. Wrap 1 bacon strip around 1 scallop and secure with a toothpick. Repeat with the remaining scallops. Season the scallops with pepper and paprika.
2. Preheat the toaster oven to 350°F.
3. Place the bacon-wrapped scallops in the air fryer oven and air-fry for 4 minutes. Cook another 6 to 7 minutes. When the bacon is crispy, the scallops should be cooked through and slightly firm, but not rubbery. Serve immediately.

Shrimp Patties

Servings: 4
Cooking Time: 10 Minutes

Ingredients:

- ½ pound shelled and deveined raw shrimp
- ¼ cup chopped red bell pepper
- ¼ cup chopped green onion
- ¼ cup chopped celery
- 2 cups cooked sushi rice
- ½ teaspoon garlic powder
- ½ teaspoon Old Bay Seasoning
- ½ teaspoon salt
- 2 teaspoons Worcestershire sauce
- ½ cup plain breadcrumbs
- oil for misting or cooking spray

Directions:

1. Finely chop the shrimp. You can do this in a food processor, but it takes only a few pulses. Be careful not to overprocess into mush.
2. Place shrimp in a large bowl and add all other ingredients except the breadcrumbs and oil. Stir until well combined.
3. Preheat the toaster oven to 390°F.
4. Shape shrimp mixture into 8 patties, no more than ½-inch thick. Roll patties in breadcrumbs and mist with oil or cooking spray.
5. Place 4 shrimp patties in air fryer oven and air-fry at 390°F for 10 minutes, until shrimp cooks through and outside is crispy.
6. Repeat step 5 to cook remaining shrimp patties.

Best-dressed Trout

Servings: 2
Cooking Time: 25 Minutes

Ingredients:

- 2 dressed trout
- 1 egg, beaten
- 2 tablespoons finely ground almonds
- 2 tablespoons unbleached flour
- 1 teaspoon paprika or smoked paprika
- Pinch of salt (optional)
- 4 lemon slices, approximately ¼ inch thick
- 1 teaspoon lemon juice

Directions:

1. Preheat the toaster oven to 400° F.
2. Brush the trout (both sides) with the beaten egg. Blend the almonds, flour, paprika, and salt in a bowl and sprinkle both sides of the trout. Insert 2 lemon slices in each trout cavity and place the trout in an oiled or nonstick 8½ × 8½ × 2-inch square baking (cake) pan.
3. BAKE for 20 minutes, or until the meat is white and firm. Remove from the oven and turn the trout carefully with a spatula.
4. BROIL for 5 minutes, or until the trout is lightly browned.

Horseradish Crusted Salmon

Servings: 2
Cooking Time: 14 Minutes

Ingredients:
- 2 (5-ounce) salmon fillets
- salt and freshly ground black pepper
- 2 teaspoons Dijon mustard
- ½ cup panko breadcrumbs
- 2 tablespoons prepared horseradish
- ½ teaspoon finely chopped lemon zest
- 1 tablespoon olive oil
- 1 tablespoon chopped fresh parsley

Directions:
1. Preheat the toaster oven to 360°F.
2. Season the salmon with salt and freshly ground black pepper. Then spread the Dijon mustard on the salmon, coating the entire surface.
3. Combine the breadcrumbs, horseradish, lemon zest and olive oil in a small bowl. Spread the mixture over the top of the salmon and press down lightly with your hands, adhering it to the salmon using the mustard as "glue".
4. Transfer the salmon to the air fryer oven and air-fry at 360°F for 14 minutes (depending on how thick your fillet is) or until the fish feels firm to the touch. Sprinkle with the parsley.

Shrimp Po'boy With Remoulade Sauce

Servings: 6

Cooking Time: 8 Minutes

Ingredients:

- ½ cup all-purpose flour
- ½ teaspoon paprika
- 1 teaspoon garlic powder
- ½ teaspoon black pepper
- ¼ teaspoon salt
- 2 eggs, whisked
- 1½ cups panko breadcrumbs
- 1 pound small shrimp, peeled and deveined
- Six 6-inch French rolls
- 2 cups shredded lettuce
- 12 ⅛-inch tomato slices
- ¾ cup Remoulade Sauce (see the following recipe)

Directions:

1. Preheat the toaster oven to 360°F.
2. In a medium bowl, mix the flour, paprika, garlic powder, pepper, and salt.
3. In a shallow dish, place the eggs.
4. In a third dish, place the panko breadcrumbs.
5. Covering the shrimp in the flour, dip them into the egg, and coat them with the breadcrumbs. Repeat until all shrimp are covered in the breading.
6. Liberally spray the metal trivet that fits inside the air fryer oven with olive oil spray. Place the shrimp onto the trivet, leaving space between the shrimp to flip. Air-fry for 4 minutes, flip the shrimp, and cook another 4 minutes. Repeat until all the shrimp are cooked.
7. Slice the rolls in half. Stuff each roll with shredded lettuce, tomato slices, breaded shrimp, and remoulade sauce. Serve immediately.

Garlic And Dill Salmon

Servings: 2

Cooking Time: 8 Minutes

Ingredients:

- 12 ounces salmon filets with skin
- 2 tablespoons melted butter
- 1 tablespoon extra-virgin olive oil
- 2 garlic cloves, minced
- 1 tablespoon fresh dill
- ½ teaspoon sea salt
- ½ lemon

Directions:

1. Pat the salmon dry with paper towels.

2. In a small bowl, mix together the melted butter, olive oil, garlic, and dill.

3. Sprinkle the top of the salmon with sea salt. Brush all sides of the salmon with the garlic and dill butter.

4. Preheat the toaster oven to 350°F.

5. Place the salmon, skin side down, in the air fryer oven. Air-fry for 6 to 8 minutes, or until the fish flakes in the center.

6. Remove the salmon and plate on a serving platter. Squeeze fresh lemon over the top of the salmon. Serve immediately.

Tuna Nuggets In Hoisin Sauce

Servings: 4

Cooking Time: 7 Minutes

Ingredients:

- ½ cup hoisin sauce
- 2 tablespoons rice wine vinegar
- 2 teaspoons sesame oil
- 1 teaspoon garlic powder
- 2 teaspoons dried lemongrass
- ¼ teaspoon red pepper flakes
- ½ small onion, quartered and thinly sliced
- 8 ounces fresh tuna, cut into 1-inch cubes
- cooking spray
- 3 cups cooked jasmine rice

Directions:

1. Mix the hoisin sauce, vinegar, sesame oil, and seasonings together.

2. Stir in the onions and tuna nuggets.

3. Spray air fryer oven baking pan with nonstick spray and pour in tuna mixture.

4. Air-fry at 390°F for 3 minutes. Stir gently.

5. Cook 2 minutes and stir again, checking for doneness. Tuna should be barely cooked through, just beginning to flake and still very moist. If necessary, continue cooking and stirring in 1-minute intervals until done.

6. Serve warm over hot jasmine rice.

Fish Sticks For Kids

Servings: 8

Cooking Time: 6 Minutes

Ingredients:

- 8 ounces fish fillets (pollock or cod)
- salt (optional)
- ½ cup plain breadcrumbs
- oil for misting or cooking spray

Directions:

1. Cut fish fillets into "fingers" about ½ x 3 inches. Sprinkle with salt to taste, if desired.
2. Roll fish in breadcrumbs. Spray all sides with oil or cooking spray.
3. Place in air fryer oven in single layer and air-fry at 390°F for 6 minutes, until golden brown and crispy.

Roasted Garlic Shrimp

Servings: 4

Cooking Time: 12 Minutes

Ingredients:

- Nonstick cooking spray
- ¼ cup unsalted butter, melted
- 2 cloves garlic, minced
- 1 teaspoon grated lemon zest
- ½ teaspoon dried thyme leaves
- ¼ teaspoon freshly ground black pepper
- Kosher salt
- 1 pound uncooked large shrimp, fresh or frozen and thawed, peeled and deveined
- 1 ½ tablespoons fresh lemon juice
- Optional: Minced fresh flat-leaf (Italian) parsley

Directions:

1. Preheat the toaster oven to 400°F. Spray a 12 x 12-inch baking pan with nonstick cooking spray.

2. Mix the melted butter, garlic, lemon zest, thyme, and pepper in a small bowl. Season with salt. Set aside.

3. Arrange the shrimp in a single layer in the prepared pan. Pour the butter mixture over the shrimp, then stir gently to coat the shrimp.

4. Roast, uncovered, for 10 to 12 minutes or until the shrimp turn pink. Drizzle with the lemon juice. Transfer to a serving platter and spoon any collected drippings over the shrimp. Garnish, if desired, with minced parsley.

Blackened Red Snapper

Servings: 4

Cooking Time: 8 Minutes

Ingredients:

- 1½ teaspoons black pepper
- ¼ teaspoon thyme
- ¼ teaspoon garlic powder
- ⅛ teaspoon cayenne pepper
- 1 teaspoon olive oil
- 4 4-ounce red snapper fillet portions, skin on
- 4 thin slices lemon
- cooking spray

Directions:

1. Mix the spices and oil together to make a paste. Rub into both sides of the fish.
2. Spray air fryer oven with nonstick cooking spray and lay snapper steaks in air fryer oven, skin-side down.
3. Place a lemon slice on each piece of fish.
4. Air-fry at 390°F for 8 minutes. The fish will not flake when done, but it should be white through the center.

Crispy Smelts

Servings: 3

Cooking Time: 20 Minutes

Ingredients:

- 1 pound Cleaned smelts
- 3 tablespoons Tapioca flour
- Vegetable oil spray
- To taste Coarse sea salt or kosher salt

Directions:

1. Preheat the toaster oven to 400°F.
2. Toss the smelts and tapioca flour in a large bowl until the little fish are evenly coated.
3. Lay the smelts out on a large cutting board. Lightly coat both sides of each fish with vegetable oil spray.
4. When the machine is at temperature, set the smelts close together in the air fryer oven, with a few even overlapping on top. Air-fry undisturbed for 20 minutes, until lightly browned and crisp.
5. Remove from the machine and turn out the fish onto a wire rack. The smelts will most likely come out as one large block, or maybe in a couple of large pieces. Cool for a minute or two, then sprinkle the smelts with salt and break the block(s) into much smaller sections or individual fish to serve.

Sweet Chili Shrimp

Servings: 4

Cooking Time: 6 Minutes

Ingredients:

- 1 pound jumbo shrimp, peeled and deveined
- ¼ cup sweet chili sauce
- 1 lime, zested and juiced
- 1 tablespoon soy sauce
- 1 tablespoon honey
- 1 tablespoon olive oil
- 1 large garlic clove, minced
- ½ teaspoon salt
- ¼ teaspoon pepper
- 1 green onion, thinly sliced, for garnish

Directions:

1. Place the shrimp in a large bowl. Whisk all the remaining ingredients except the green onion in a separate bowl.
2. Pour sauce over the shrimp and toss to coat.
3. Preheat the toaster Oven to 430°F.
4. Line the food tray with foil, place shrimp on the tray, then insert at top position in the preheated oven.
5. Select the Air Fry function, adjust time to 6 minutes, and press Start/Pause.
6. Remove shrimp and garnish with sliced green onions.

Lobster Tails

Servings: 4

Cooking Time: 10 Minutes

Ingredients:

- Brushing mixture:
- 2 tablespoons lemon juice
- 2 tablespoons olive oil
- ½ teaspoon garlic powder
- ¼ teaspoon ground thyme
- 4 6-ounce lobster tails

Directions:

1. Whisk together the brushing mixture ingredients in a small bowl and set aside. CUT the top of each lobster shell lengthwise from the top edge to the tail with a sharp scissors. Place the lobster tails, cut side down, on a broiling rack with a pan underneath. Brush with the brushing mixture.
2. BROIL for 5 minutes. Remove from the oven and brush again. Broil for 5 minutes, or until the lobster flesh turns from translucent to opaque.

Flounder Fillets

Servings: 4
Cooking Time: 8 Minutes

Ingredients:

- 1 egg white
- 1 tablespoon water
- 1 cup panko breadcrumbs
- 2 tablespoons extra-light virgin olive oil
- 4 4-ounce flounder fillets
- salt and pepper
- oil for misting or cooking spray

Directions:

1. Preheat the toaster oven to 390°F.
2. Beat together egg white and water in shallow dish.
3. In another shallow dish, mix panko crumbs and oil until well combined and crumbly (best done by hand).
4. Season flounder fillets with salt and pepper to taste. Dip each fillet into egg mixture and then roll in panko crumbs, pressing in crumbs so that fish is nicely coated.
5. Spray air fryer oven with nonstick cooking spray and add fillets. Air-fry at 390°F for 3 minutes.
6. Spray fish fillets but do not turn. Cook 5 minutes longer or until golden brown and crispy. Using a spatula, carefully remove fish from air fryer oven and serve.

BEEF PORK AND LAMB

Barbecued Broiled Pork Chops

Servings: 2
Cooking Time: 16 Minutes

Ingredients:

- Barbecue sauce mixture:
- 1 tablespoon ketchup
- ¼ cup dry red wine
- 1 tablespoon vegetable oil
- ⅛ teaspoon smoked flavoring (liquid smoke)
- 1 teaspoon chili powder
- 1 teaspoon ground cumin
- 1 teaspoon brown sugar
- ¼ teaspoon butcher's pepper
- 2 large (6- to 8-ounce) lean pork chops, approximately ¾ to 1 inch thick

Directions:

1. Combine the barbecue sauce mixture ingredients in a small bowl. Brush the chops with the sauce and place on a broiling rack with a pan underneath.
2. BROIL 8 minutes, turn with tongs, and broil for another 8 minutes, or until the meat is cooked to your preference.

Seasoned Boneless Pork Sirloin Chops

Servings: 2
Cooking Time: 16 Minutes

Ingredients:

- Seasoning mixture:
- ½ teaspoon ground cumin
- ¼ teaspoon turmeric
- Pinch of ground cardamom
- Pinch of grated nutmeg
- 1 teaspoon vegetable oil
- 1 teaspoon Pickapeppa sauce
- 2½- to ¾-pound boneless lean pork sirloin chops

Directions:

1. Combine the seasoning mixture ingredients in a small bowl and brush on both sides of the chops. Place the chops on the broiling rack with a pan underneath.
2. BROIL 8 minutes, remove the chops, turn, and brush with the mixture. Broil again for 8 minutes, or until the chops are done to your preference.

California Burritos

Servings: 4

Cooking Time: 17 Minutes

Ingredients:

- 1 pound sirloin steak, sliced thin
- 1 teaspoon dried oregano
- 1 teaspoon ground cumin
- ½ teaspoon garlic powder
- 16 tater tots
- ⅓ cup sour cream
- ½ lime, juiced
- 2 tablespoons hot sauce
- 1 large avocado, pitted
- 1 teaspoon salt, divided
- 4 large (8- to 10-inch) flour tortillas
- ½ cup shredded cheddar cheese or Monterey jack
- 2 tablespoons avocado oil

Directions:

1. Preheat the toaster oven to 380°F.

2. Season the steak with oregano, cumin, and garlic powder. Place the steak on one side of the air fryer oven and the tater tots on the other side. (It's okay for them to touch, because the flavors will all come together in the burrito.) Air-fry for 8 minutes, toss, and cook an additional 4 to 6 minutes.

3. Meanwhile, in a small bowl, stir together the sour cream, lime juice, and hot sauce.

4. In another small bowl, mash together the avocado and season with ½ teaspoon of the salt, to taste.

5. To assemble the burrito, lay out the tortillas, equally divide the meat amongst the tortillas. Season the steak equally with the remaining ½ teaspoon salt. Then layer the mashed avocado and sour cream mixture on top. Top each tortilla with 4 tater tots and finish each with 2 tablespoons cheese. Roll up the sides and, while holding in the sides, roll up the burrito. Place the burritos in the air fryer oven and brush with avocado oil (working in batches as needed); air-fry for 3 minutes or until lightly golden on the outside.

Beef, Onion, And Pepper Shish Kebab

Servings: 4

Cooking Time: 20 Minutes

Ingredients:

- Marinade:
- 2 tablespoons olive oil
- ½ cup dry red wine
- 1 tablespoon soy sauce
- 1 teaspoon chili powder
- 1 teaspoon Worcestershire sauce
- 1 teaspoon garlic powder
- 1 teaspoon spicy brown mustard
- 1 teaspoon brown sugar
- 8 onion quarters, approximately 2 × 2-inch pieces
- 8 bell pepper quarters, 2 × 2-inch pieces
- 1 pound lean boneless beef (sirloin, round steak, London broil), cut into 8 2-inch cubes
- 4 8-inch metal or wooden (bamboo) skewers

Directions:

1. Combine the marinade ingredients in a large bowl. Add the onion, peppers, and beef. Refrigerate, covered, for at least 1 hour or

2. Skewer alternating beef, pepper, and onion pieces. Brush with the marinade mixture and place the skewers on a broiling rack with the pan underneath.

3. BROIL for 5 minutes, remove the pan with the skewers from the oven, turn the skewers, brush again, then broil for another 5 minutes. Repeat turning and brushing every 5 minutes, until the peppers and onions are well cooked and browned to your preference.

Cilantro-crusted Flank Steak

Servings: 2

Cooking Time: 16 Minutes

Ingredients:

- Coating:
- 2 tablespoons chopped onion
- 1 tablespoon olive oil
- 2 tablespoons plain nonfat yogurt
- 1 plum tomato
- ½ cup fresh cilantro leaves
- 2 tablespoons cooking sherry
- ¼ teaspoon hot sauce
- 1 teaspoon garlic powder
- ½ teaspoon chili powder
- Salt and freshly ground black pepper
- 2 8-ounce flank steaks

Directions:

1. Process the coating ingredients in a blender or food processor until smooth. Spread half of the coating mixture on top of the flank steaks. Place the steaks on a broiling rack with a pan underneath.

2. BROIL for 8 minutes. Turn with tongs, spread the remaining mixture on the steaks, and broil again for 8 minutes, or until done to your preference.

Mustard-herb Lamb Chops

Servings: 2

Cooking Time: 15 Minutes

Ingredients:

- 2 tablespoons Dijon mustard
- 1 teaspoon minced garlic
- ¼ cup bread crumbs
- 1 teaspoon dried Italian herbs
- Zest of 1 lemon
- 4 lamb loin chops (about 1 pound), room temperature
- Sea salt, for seasoning
- Freshly ground black pepper, for seasoning
- Oil spray (hand-pumped)

Directions:

1. Preheat the toaster oven to 425°F on CONVECTION BAKE for 5 minutes.
2. Line the baking tray with parchment or aluminum foil.
3. In a small bowl, stir the mustard and garlic until blended.
4. In another small bowl, stir the bread crumbs, herbs, and lemon zest until mixed.
5. Lightly season the lamb chops on both sides with salt and pepper. Brush the mustard mixture over a chop and dredge it in the bread crumb mixture to lightly bread the lamb. Set the lamb on the baking tray and repeat with the other chops.
6. Spray the chops lightly with the oil, and in position 2, bake for 15 minutes until browned and the internal temperature is 130°F for medium-rare.
7. Rest the lamb for 5 minutes, then serve.

Vietnamese Beef Lettuce Wraps

Servings: 4

Cooking Time: 12 Minutes

Ingredients:

- ⅓ cup low-sodium soy sauce
- 2 teaspoons fish sauce
- 2 teaspoons brown sugar
- 1 tablespoon chili paste
- juice of 1 lime
- 2 cloves garlic, minced
- 2 teaspoons fresh ginger, minced
- 1 pound beef sirloin
- Sauce
- ⅓ cup low-sodium soy sauce

- juice of 2 limes
- 1 tablespoon mirin wine
- 2 teaspoons chili paste
- Serving
- 1 head butter lettuce
- ½ cup julienned carrots
- ½ cup julienned cucumber
- ½ cup sliced radishes, sliced into half moons
- 2 cups cooked rice noodles
- ⅓ cup chopped peanuts

Directions:

1. Combine the soy sauce, fish sauce, brown sugar, chili paste, lime juice, garlic and ginger in a bowl. Slice the beef into thin slices, then cut those slices in half. Add the beef to the marinade and marinate for 1 to 3 hours in the refrigerator. When you are ready to cook, remove the steak from the refrigerator and let it sit at room temperature for 30 minutes.

2. Preheat the toaster oven to 400°F.

3. Transfer the beef and marinade to the air fryer oven. Air-fry at 400°F for 12 minutes.

4. While the beef is cooking, prepare a wrap-building station. Combine the soy sauce, lime juice, mirin wine and chili paste in a bowl and transfer to a little pouring vessel. Separate the lettuce leaves from the head of lettuce and put them in a serving bowl. Place the carrots, cucumber, radish, rice noodles and chopped peanuts all in separate serving bowls.

5. When the beef has finished cooking, transfer it to another serving bowl and invite your guests to build their wraps. To build the wraps, place some beef in a lettuce leaf and top with carrots, cucumbers, some rice noodles and chopped peanuts. Drizzle a little sauce over top, fold the lettuce around the ingredients and enjoy!

Herbed Lamb Burgers

Servings: 4
Cooking Time: 15 Minutes

Ingredients:

- 1 pound lean ground lamb
- 1 large egg
- 1 tablespoon fresh parsley, chopped
- 2 teaspoons fresh mint, chopped
- 1 teaspoon minced garlic
- ¼ teaspoon sea salt
- ⅛ teaspoon freshly ground black pepper
- Olive oil spray (hand-pumped)
- 4 whole-wheat buns
- ¼ cup store-bought tzatziki sauce
- 1 tomato, cut into slices
- 4 thin red onion slices
- ½ cup shredded lettuce

Directions:

1. Preheat the toaster oven to 350°F on CONVECTION BROIL for 5 minutes.
2. In a large bowl, mix the lamb, egg, parsley, mint, garlic, salt, and pepper. Form the mixture into 4 patties.
3. Place the air-fryer basket in the baking tray and place the burger patties in the basket. Lightly spray the patties with the oil on both sides.
4. In position 2, broil for 15 minutes, turning halfway through.
5. Serve on the buns topped with tzatziki sauce, tomato, onion, and lettuce.

Spicy Flank Steak With Fresh Tomato-corn Salsa

Servings: 4

Cooking Time: 20 Minutes

Ingredients:

- 2 large tomatoes, chopped
- 1 cup fresh (or canned) corn
- ½ English cucumber, chopped
- ¼ red onion, chopped
- 1 tablespoon jalapeño pepper, chopped
- 1 tablespoon fresh cilantro, chopped
- Sea salt, for seasoning
- Freshly ground black pepper, for seasoning
- 1 pound extra-lean beef flank steak, trimmed of fat
- Olive oil, for brushing
- 1 teaspoon garlic powder
- 1 teaspoon chili powder

Directions:

1. Preheat the toaster oven to 450°F on BROIL for 5 minutes.
2. In a small bowl, stir the tomato, corn, cucumber, onion, jalapeño, and cilantro, and season with salt and pepper.
3. Rub the steak all over with the oil and then season with garlic powder, chili powder, salt, and pepper.
4. Place the air-fryer basket in the baking tray and arrange the steak in the basket.
5. In position 2, broil for 20 minutes, turning halfway through, until browned and with an internal temperature of 140°F, for medium-rare.
6. Let the steak rest for 10 minutes and then cut it very thinly against the grain.
7. Serve with the salsa.

Air-fried Roast Beef With Rosemary Roasted Potatoes

Servings: 8

Cooking Time: 60 Minutes

Ingredients:

- 1 (5-pound) top sirloin roast
- salt and freshly ground black pepper
- 1 teaspoon dried thyme
- 2 pounds red potatoes, halved or quartered
- 2 teaspoons olive oil
- 1 teaspoon very finely chopped fresh rosemary, plus more for garnish

Directions:

1. Start by making sure your roast will fit into the air fryer oven without touching the top element. Trim it if you have to in order to get it to fit nicely in your air fryer oven. (You can always save the trimmings for another use, like a beef sandwich.)
2. Preheat the toaster oven to 360°F.
3. Season the beef all over with salt, pepper and thyme. Transfer the seasoned roast to the air fryer oven.
4. Air-fry at 360°F for 20 minutes. Turn the roast over and continue to air-fry at 360°F for another 20 minutes.
5. Toss the potatoes with the olive oil, salt, pepper and fresh rosemary. Turn the roast over again in the air fryer oven and toss the potatoes in around the sides of the roast. Air-fry the roast and potatoes at 360°F for another 20 minutes. Check the internal temperature of the roast with an instant-read thermometer, and continue to roast until the beef is 5° lower than your desired degree of doneness. (Rare – 130°F, Medium – 150°F, Well done – 170°F.) Let the roast rest for 5 to 10 minutes before slicing and serving. While the roast is resting, continue to air-fry the potatoes if desired for extra browning and crispiness.
6. Slice the roast and serve with the potatoes, adding a little more fresh rosemary if desired.

Stuffed Bell Peppers

Servings: 4
Cooking Time: 10 Minutes

Ingredients:

- ¼ pound lean ground pork
- ¾ pound lean ground beef
- ¼ cup onion, minced
- 1 15-ounce can Red Gold crushed tomatoes
- 1 teaspoon Worcestershire sauce
- 1 teaspoon barbeque seasoning
- 1 teaspoon honey
- ½ teaspoon dried basil
- ½ cup cooked brown rice
- ½ teaspoon garlic powder
- ½ teaspoon oregano
- ½ teaspoon salt
- 2 small bell peppers

Directions:

1. Place pork, beef, and onion in air fryer oven baking pan and air-fry at 360°F for 5 minutes.
2. Stir to break apart chunks and cook 3 more minutes. Continue cooking and stirring in 2-minute intervals until meat is well done. Remove from pan and drain.
3. In a small saucepan, combine the tomatoes, Worcestershire, barbeque seasoning, honey, and basil. Stir well to mix in honey and seasonings.
4. In a large bowl, combine the cooked meat mixture, rice, garlic powder, oregano, and salt. Add ¼ cup of the seasoned crushed tomatoes. Stir until well mixed.
5. Cut peppers in half and remove stems and seeds.
6. Stuff each pepper half with one fourth of the meat mixture.
7. Place the peppers in air fryer oven and air-fry for 10 minutes, until peppers are crisp tender.
8. Heat remaining tomato sauce. Serve peppers with warm sauce spooned over top.

Better-than-chinese-take-out Pork Ribs

Servings: 3

Cooking Time: 35 Minutes

Ingredients:
- 1½ tablespoons Hoisin sauce (gluten-free, if a concern)
- 1½ tablespoons Regular or low-sodium soy sauce or gluten-free tamari sauce
- 1½ tablespoons Shaoxing (Chinese cooking rice wine), dry sherry, or white grape juice
- 1½ teaspoons Minced garlic
- ¾ teaspoon Ground dried ginger
- ¾ teaspoon Ground white pepper
- 1½ pounds Pork baby back rib rack(s), cut into 2-bone pieces

Directions:

1. Mix the hoisin sauce, soy or tamari sauce, Shaoxing or its substitute, garlic, ginger, and white pepper in a large bowl. Add the rib sections and stir well to coat. Cover and refrigerate for at least 2 hours or up to 24 hours, stirring the rib sections in the marinade occasionally.

2. Preheat the toaster oven to 350°F . Set the ribs in their bowl on the counter as the machine heats.

3. When the machine is at temperature, set the rib pieces on their sides in a single layer in the air fryer oven with as much air space between them as possible. Air-fry for 35 minutes, turning and rearranging the pieces once, until deeply browned and sizzling.

4. Use kitchen tongs to transfer the rib pieces to a large serving bowl or platter. Wait a minute or two before serving them so the meat can reabsorb some of its own juices.

Barbecue-style London Broil

Servings: 5

Cooking Time: 17 Minutes

Ingredients:

- ¾ teaspoon Mild smoked paprika
- ¾ teaspoon Dried oregano
- ¾ teaspoon Table salt
- ¾ teaspoon Ground black pepper
- ¼ teaspoon Garlic powder
- ¼ teaspoon Onion powder
- 1½ pounds Beef London broil (in one piece)
- Olive oil spray

Directions:

1. Preheat the toaster oven to 400°F.

2. Mix the smoked paprika, oregano, salt, pepper, garlic powder, and onion powder in a small bowl until uniform.

3. Pat and rub this mixture across all surfaces of the beef. Lightly coat the beef on all sides with olive oil spray.

4. When the machine is at temperature, lay the London broil flat in the air fryer oven and air-fry undisturbed for 8 minutes for the small batch, 10 minutes for the medium batch, or 12 minutes for the large batch for medium-rare, until an instant-read meat thermometer inserted into the center of the meat registers 130°F (not USDA-approved). Add 1, 2, or 3 minutes, respectively (based on the size of the cut) for medium, until an instant-read meat thermometer registers 135°F (not USDA-approved). Or add 3, 4, or 5 minutes respectively for medium, until an instant-read meat thermometer registers 145°F (USDA-approved).

5. Use kitchen tongs to transfer the London broil to a cutting board. Let the meat rest for 10 minutes. It needs a long time for the juices to be reincorporated into the meat's fibers. Carve it against the grain into very thin (less than ¼-inch-thick) slices to serve.

Lime And Cumin Lamb Kebabs

Servings: 4

Cooking Time: 16 Minutes

Ingredients:

- 1 pound boneless lean lamb, trimmed and cut into 1 × 1-inch pieces
- 2 plum tomatoes, cut into 2 × 2-inch pieces
- 1 bell pepper, cut into 2 × 2-inch pieces
- 1 small onion, cut into 2 × 2-inch pieces
- Brushing mixture:
- ¼ cup lime juice
- ½ teaspoon soy sauce
- 1 tablespoon honey
- 1½ teaspoon ground cumin

Directions:

1. Skewer alternating pieces of lamb, tomato, pepper, and onion on four 9-inch skewers.
2. Combine the brushing mixture ingredients in a small bowl and brush on the kebabs. Place the skewers on a broiling rack with a pan underneath.
3. BROIL for 8 minutes. Turn the skewers, brush the kebabs with the mixture, and broil for 8 minutes, or until the meat and vegetables are cooked and browned.

Ribeye Steak With Blue Cheese Compound Butter

Servings: 2

Cooking Time: 12 Minutes

Ingredients:

- 5 tablespoons unsalted butter, softened
- ¼ cup crumbled blue cheese 2 teaspoons lemon juice
- 1 tablespoon freshly chopped chives
- Salt & freshly ground black pepper, to taste
- 2 (12 ounce) boneless ribeye steaks

Directions:

1. Mix together butter, blue cheese, lemon juice, and chives until smooth.
2. Season the butter to taste with salt and pepper.
3. Place the butter on plastic wrap and form into a 3-inch log, tying the ends of the plastic wrap together.
4. Place the butter in the fridge for 4 hours to harden.
5. Allow the steaks to sit at room temperature for 1 hour.
6. Pat the steaks dry with paper towels and season to taste with salt and pepper.
7. Insert the fry basket at top position in the Cosori Smart Air Fryer Toaster Oven.
8. Preheat the toaster Oven to 450°F.
9. Place the steaks in the fry basket in the preheated oven.
10. Select the Broil function, adjust time to 12 minutes, and press Start/Pause.
11. Remove when done and allow to rest for 5 minutes.
12. Remove the butter from the fridge, unwrap, and slice into ¾-inch pieces.
13. Serve the steak with one or two pieces of sliced compound butter.

Lime-ginger Pork Tenderloin

Servings: 4

Cooking Time: 26 Minutes

Ingredients:

- ½ cup packed dark brown sugar
- Juice of ½ lime
- 2 teaspoons fresh ginger, peeled and grated
- 1 teaspoon minced garlic
- 2 (1-pound) extra-lean pork tenderloins, trimmed of fat
- Sea salt, for seasoning
- Freshly ground black pepper, for seasoning
- 1 tablespoon olive oil

Directions:

1. Preheat the toaster oven to 400°F on CONVECTION BAKE for 5 minutes.
2. In a small bowl, stir the sugar, lime juice, ginger, and garlic together.
3. Lightly season the pork tenderloins all over with salt and pepper.
4. Heat the oil in a large skillet over medium-high heat. Brown the pork on all sides, about 6 minutes in total.
5. Place the air-fryer basket in the baking tray and place the tenderloins in the basket.
6. Brush the pork all over with the ginger-lime mixture.
7. In position 2, bake for 20 minutes, basting the pork at 10 minutes, until it reaches an internal temperature of about 145°F.
8. Let the pork rest for 10 minutes and serve.

Calf's Liver

Servings: 4
Cooking Time: 5 Minutes

Ingredients:

- 1 pound sliced calf's liver
- salt and pepper
- 2 eggs
- 2 tablespoons milk
- ½ cup whole wheat flour
- 1½ cups panko breadcrumbs
- ½ cup plain breadcrumbs
- ½ teaspoon salt
- ¼ teaspoon pepper
- oil for misting or cooking spray

Directions:

1. Cut liver slices crosswise into strips about ½-inch wide. Sprinkle with salt and pepper to taste.
2. Beat together egg and milk in a shallow dish.
3. Place wheat flour in a second shallow dish.
4. In a third shallow dish, mix together panko, plain breadcrumbs, ½ teaspoon salt, and ¼ teaspoon pepper.
5. Preheat the toaster oven to 390°F.
6. Dip liver strips in flour, egg wash, and then breadcrumbs, pressing in coating slightly to make crumbs stick.
7. Cooking half the liver at a time, place strips in air fryer oven in a single layer, close but not touching. Air-fry at 390°F for 5 minutes or until done to your preference.
8. Repeat step 7 to cook remaining liver.

Crispy Smoked Pork Chops

Servings: 3

Cooking Time: 8 Minutes

Ingredients:
- ⅔ cup All-purpose flour or tapioca flour
- 1 Large egg white(s)
- 2 tablespoons Water
- 1½ cups Corn flake crumbs (gluten-free, if a concern)
- 3 ½-pound, ½-inch-thick bone-in smoked pork chops

Directions:
1. Preheat the toaster oven to 375°F.
2. Set up and fill three shallow soup plates or small pie plates on your counter: one for the flour; one for the egg white(s), whisked with the water until foamy; and one for the corn flake crumbs.
3. Set a chop in the flour and turn it several times, coating both sides and the edges. Gently shake off any excess flour, then set it in the beaten egg white mixture. Turn to coat both sides as well as the edges. Let any excess egg white slip back into the rest, then set the chop in the corn flake crumbs. Turn it several times, pressing gently to coat the chop evenly on both sides and around the edge. Set the chop aside and continue coating the remaining chop(s) in the same way.
4. Set the chops in the air fryer oven with as much air space between them as possible. Air-fry undisturbed for 8 minutes, or until the coating is crunchy and the chops are heated through.
5. Use kitchen tongs to transfer the chops to a wire rack and cool for a couple of minutes before serving.

Pork Cutlets With Almond-lemon Crust

Servings: 3

Cooking Time: 14 Minutes

Ingredients:

- ¾ cup Almond flour
- ¾ cup Plain dried bread crumbs (gluten-free, if a concern)
- 1½ teaspoons Finely grated lemon zest
- 1¼ teaspoons Table salt
- ¾ teaspoon Garlic powder
- ¾ teaspoon Dried oregano
- 1 Large egg white(s)
- 2 tablespoons Water
- 3 6-ounce center-cut boneless pork loin chops (about ¾ inch thick)
- Olive oil spray

Directions:

1. Preheat the toaster oven to 375°F .

2. Mix the almond flour, bread crumbs, lemon zest, salt, garlic powder, and dried oregano in a large bowl until well combined.

3. Whisk the egg white(s) and water in a shallow soup plate or small pie plate until uniform.

4. Dip a chop in the egg white mixture, turning it to coat all sides, even the ends. Let any excess egg white mixture slip back into the rest, then set it in the almond flour mixture. Turn it several times, pressing gently to coat it evenly. Generously coat the chop with olive oil spray, then set aside to dip and coat the remaining chop(s).

5. Set the chops in the air fryer oven with as much air space between them as possible. Air-fry undisturbed for 12 minutes, or until browned and crunchy. You may need to add 2 minutes to the cooking time if the machine is at 360°F.

6. Use kitchen tongs to transfer the chops to a wire rack. Cool for a few minutes before serving.

POULTRY

Chicken Parmesan

Servings: 4
Cooking Time: 11 Minutes

Ingredients:

- 4 chicken tenders
- Italian seasoning
- salt
- ¼ cup cornstarch
- ½ cup Italian salad dressing
- ¼ cup panko breadcrumbs
- ¼ cup grated Parmesan cheese, plus more for serving
- oil for misting or cooking spray
- 8 ounces spaghetti, cooked
- 1 24-ounce jar marinara sauce

Directions:

1. Pound chicken tenders with meat mallet or rolling pin until about ¼-inch thick.
2. Sprinkle both sides with Italian seasoning and salt to taste.
3. Place cornstarch and salad dressing in 2 separate shallow dishes.
4. In a third shallow dish, mix together the panko crumbs and Parmesan cheese.
5. Dip flattened chicken in cornstarch, then salad dressing. Dip in the panko mixture, pressing into the chicken so the coating sticks well.
6. Spray both sides with oil or cooking spray. Place in air fryer oven in single layer.
7. Air-fry at 390°F for 5 minutes. Spray with oil again, turning chicken to coat both sides. See tip about turning.
8. Air-fry for an additional 6 minutes or until chicken juices run clear and outside is browned.
9. While chicken is cooking, heat marinara sauce and stir into cooked spaghetti.
10. To serve, divide spaghetti with sauce among 4 dinner plates, and top each with a fried chicken tender. Pass additional Parmesan at the table for those who want extra cheese.

Orange-glazed Roast Chicken

Servings: 6
Cooking Time: 100 Minutes

Ingredients:

- 1 3-pound whole chicken, rinsed and patted dry with paper towels
- Brushing mixture:
- 2 tablespoons orange juice concentrate
- 1 tablespoon soy sauce
- 1 tablespoon toasted sesame oil
- 1 teaspoon ground ginger
- Salt and freshly ground black pepper to taste

Directions:

1. Preheat the toaster oven to 400° F.
2. Place the chicken, breast side up, in an oiled or nonstick 8½ × 8½ × 2-inch square (cake) pan and brush with the mixture, which has been combined in a small bowl, reserving the remaining mixture. Cover with aluminum foil.
3. BAKE for 1 hour and 20 minutes. Uncover and brush the chicken with remaining mixture.
4. BAKE, uncovered, for 20 minutes, or until the breast is tender when pierced with a fork and golden brown.

Sticky Soy Chicken Thighs

Servings: 2
Cooking Time: 20 Minutes

Ingredients:

- 2 tablespoons less-sodium soy sauce
- 1 tablespoon olive oil
- 1 tablespoon honey
- 1 tablespoon balsamic vinegar
- 1 tablespoon chili sauce
- Juice of 1 lime
- 1 teaspoon minced garlic
- 1 teaspoon ginger, peeled and grated
- 2 bone-in, skin-on chicken thighs
- Oil spray (hand-pumped)
- 1 scallion, both white and green parts, thinly sliced, for garnish
- 2 teaspoons sesame seeds, for garnish

Directions:

1. Preheat the toaster oven to 400°F on AIR FRY for 5 minutes.
2. In a large bowl, combine the soy sauce, olive oil, honey, balsamic vinegar, chili sauce, lime juice, garlic, and ginger. Add the chicken thighs to the bowl and toss to coat. Cover the bowl and refrigerate for 30 minutes.
3. Place the air-fryer basket in the baking tray and generously spray with oil.
4. Place the thighs in the basket, and in position 2, air fry for 20 minutes until cooked through and the thighs are browned and lightly caramelized, with an internal temperature of 165°F.
5. Garnish the chicken with the scallion and sesame seeds and serve.

Pesto-crusted Chicken

Servings: 2

Cooking Time: 31 Minutes

Ingredients:
- Pesto:
- 1 cup fresh cilantro, parsley, and basil leaves
- 3 tablespoons nonfat plain yogurt
- ¼ cup pine nuts, walnut, or pecans
- 3 tablespoons grated Parmesan cheese
- 2 peeled garlic cloves
- 1 tablespoon lemon juice
- 3 tablespoons olive oil
- Salt and freshly ground black pepper to taste
- 2 skinless, boneless chicken breast halves

Directions:
1. Preheat the toaster oven to 450° F.
2. Blend the pesto ingredients in a blender or food processor until smooth. Set aside.
3. Place the chicken breast halves in an oiled or nonstick 8½ × 8½ × 2-inch square (cake) pan. With a butter knife or spatula, spread the mixture liberally on both sides of each chicken breast. Cover the dish with aluminum foil.
4. BAKE, covered, for 25 minutes, or until the chicken is tender. Remove from the oven and uncover.
5. BROIL for 6 minutes, or until the pesto coating is lightly browned.

Guiltless Bacon

Servings: 4

Cooking Time: 10 Minutes

Ingredients:
- 6 slices lean turkey bacon, placed on a broiling pan

Directions:
1. BROIL 5 minutes, turn the pieces, and broil again for 5 more minutes, or until done to your preference. Press the slices between paper towels and serve immediately.

Roasted Game Hens With Vegetable Stuffing

Servings: 2

Cooking Time: 50 Minutes

Ingredients:

- Stuffing:
- 1 cup multigrain bread crumbs
- 2 tablespoons chopped onion
- 1 carrot, shredded
- 1 celery stalk, shredded
- 1 garlic clove, minced
- 2 tablespoons chopped fresh parsley
- Salt and freshly ground black pepper to taste
- 2 whole game hens (thawed or fresh), giblets removed, rinsed, and patted dry with paper towels

Directions:

1. Preheat the toaster oven to 350° F.

2. Combine the stuffing ingredients in a medium bowl. Stuff the cavities of the game hens and place them in a baking dish.

3. BAKE, covered, for 45 minutes, or until the meat is tender and the juices run clear when the breast is pierced with a fork.

4. BROIL, uncovered, for 8 minutes, or until lightly browned.

Light And Lovely Loaf

Servings: 4

Cooking Time: 30 Minutes

Ingredients:

- 2 cups ground chicken or turkey breast
- 1 egg
- ½ cup grated carrot
- ½ cup grated celery
- 1 tablespoon finely chopped onion
- ½ teaspoon garlic powder
- Salt and freshly ground black pepper to taste

Directions:

1. Preheat the toaster oven to 400° F.

2. Blend all ingredients in a bowl, mixing well, and transfer to an oiled or nonstick regular-size 4½ × 8½ × 2¼-inch loaf pan

3. BAKE, uncovered, for 30 minutes, until lightly browned.

Peanut Butter-barbeque Chicken

Servings: 4
Cooking Time: 20 Minutes

Ingredients:

- 1 pound boneless, skinless chicken thighs
- salt and pepper
- 1 large orange
- ½ cup barbeque sauce
- 2 tablespoons smooth peanut butter
- 2 tablespoons chopped peanuts for garnish (optional)
- cooking spray

Directions:

1. Season chicken with salt and pepper to taste. Place in a shallow dish or plastic bag.
2. Grate orange peel, squeeze orange and reserve 1 tablespoon of juice for the sauce.
3. Pour remaining juice over chicken and marinate for 30 minutes.
4. Mix together the reserved 1 tablespoon of orange juice, barbeque sauce, peanut butter, and 1 teaspoon grated orange peel.
5. Place ¼ cup of sauce mixture in a small bowl for basting. Set remaining sauce aside to serve with cooked chicken.
6. Preheat the toaster oven to 360°F. Spray air fryer oven with nonstick cooking spray.
7. Remove chicken from marinade, letting excess drip off. Place in air fryer oven and air-fry for 5 minutes. Turn chicken over and cook 5 minutes longer.
8. Brush both sides of chicken lightly with sauce.
9. Cook chicken 5 minutes, then turn thighs one more time, again brushing both sides lightly with sauce. Air-fry for 5 more minutes or until chicken is done and juices run clear.
10. Serve chicken with remaining sauce on the side and garnish with chopped peanuts if you like.

Chicken In Mango Sauce

Servings: 2
Cooking Time: 40 Minutes

Ingredients:

- 2 skinless and boneless chicken breast halves
- 1 tablespoon capers
- 1 tablespoon raisins
- Mango mixture:
- 1 cup mango pieces
- 1 teaspoon balsamic vinegar
- ½ teaspoon garlic powder
- 1 teaspoon fresh ginger, peeled and minced
- ½ teaspoon soy sauce
- ½ teaspoon curry powder
- 1 tablespoon pimientos, minced
- Salt and pepper to taste

Directions:

1. Preheat the toaster oven to 375° F.
2. Process the mango mixture ingredients in a food processor or blender until smooth. Transfer to an oiled or nonstick 8½ × 8½ × 2-inch square (cake) pan and add the capers, raisins, and pimientos, stirring well to blend. Add the chicken breasts and spoon the mixture over the breasts to coat well.
3. BAKE for 40 minutes. Serve the breasts with the sauce.

Buffalo Egg Rolls

Servings: 8
Cooking Time: 9 Minutes

Ingredients:

- 1 teaspoon water
- 1 tablespoon cornstarch
- 1 egg
- 2½ cups cooked chicken, diced or shredded (see opposite page)
- ⅓ cup chopped green onion
- ⅓ cup diced celery
- ⅓ cup buffalo wing sauce
- 8 egg roll wraps
- oil for misting or cooking spray
- Blue Cheese Dip
- 3 ounces cream cheese, softened
- ⅓ cup blue cheese, crumbled
- 1 teaspoon Worcestershire sauce
- ¼ teaspoon garlic powder
- ¼ cup buttermilk (or sour cream)

Directions:

1. Mix water and cornstarch in a small bowl until dissolved. Add egg, beat well, and set aside.
2. In a medium size bowl, mix together chicken, green onion, celery, and buffalo wing sauce.
3. Divide chicken mixture evenly among 8 egg roll wraps, spooning ½ inch from one edge.
4. Moisten all edges of each wrap with beaten egg wash.
5. Fold the short ends over filling, then roll up tightly and press to seal edges.
6. Brush outside of wraps with egg wash, then spritz with oil or cooking spray.
7. Place 4 egg rolls in air fryer oven.
8. Air-fry at 390°F for 9 minutes or until outside is brown and crispy.
9. While the rolls are cooking, prepare the Blue Cheese Dip. With a fork, mash together cream cheese and blue cheese.
10. Stir in remaining ingredients.
11. Dip should be just thick enough to slightly cling to egg rolls. If too thick, stir in buttermilk or milk 1 tablespoon at a time until you reach the desired consistency.
12. Cook remaining 4 egg rolls as in steps 7 and 8.
13. Serve while hot with Blue Cheese Dip, more buffalo wing sauce, or both.

Chicken Pot Pie

Servings: 4

Cooking Time: 65 Minutes

Ingredients:

- ¼ cup salted butter
- 1 small sweet onion, chopped
- 1 carrot, chopped
- 1 teaspoon minced garlic
- ¼ cup all-purpose flour
- 1 cup low-sodium chicken broth
- ¼ cup heavy (whipping) cream
- 2 cups diced store-bought rotisserie chicken
- 1 cup frozen peas
- Sea salt, for seasoning
- Freshly ground black pepper, for seasoning
- 1 unbaked store-bought pie crust

Directions:

1. Place the rack in position 1 and preheat the toaster oven to 350°F on BAKE for 5 minutes.

2. Melt the butter in a large saucepan over medium-high heat. Sauté the onion, carrot, and garlic until softened, about 12 minutes. Whisk in the flour to form a thick paste and whisk for 1 minute to cook.

3. Add the broth and whisk until thickened, about 2 minutes. Add the heavy cream, whisking to combine. Add the chicken and peas, and season with salt and pepper.

4. Transfer the filling to a 1½-quart casserole dish and top with the pie crust, tucking the edges into the sides of the casserole dish to completely enclose the filling. Cut 4 or 5 slits in the top of the crust.

5. Bake for 50 minutes until the crust is golden brown and the filling is bubbly. Serve.

Gluten-free Nutty Chicken Fingers

Servings: 4

Cooking Time: 10 Minutes

Ingredients:

- ½ cup gluten-free flour
- ½ teaspoon garlic powder
- ¼ teaspoon onion powder
- ¼ teaspoon black pepper
- ¼ teaspoon salt
- 1 cup walnuts, pulsed into coarse flour
- ½ cup gluten-free breadcrumbs
- 2 large eggs
- 1 pound boneless, skinless chicken tenders

Directions:

1. Preheat the toaster oven to 400°F.
2. In a medium bowl, mix the flour, garlic, onion, pepper, and salt. Set aside.
3. In a separate bowl, mix the walnut flour and breadcrumbs.
4. In a third bowl, whisk the eggs.
5. Liberally spray the air fryer oven with olive oil spray.
6. Pat the chicken tenders dry with a paper towel. Dredge the tenders one at a time in the flour, then dip them in the egg, and toss them in the breadcrumb coating. Repeat until all tenders are coated.
7. Set each tender in the air fryer oven, leaving room on each side of the tender to allow for flipping.
8. When the air fryer oven is full, cook 5 minutes, flip, and cook another 5 minutes. Check the internal temperature after cooking completes; it should read 165°F. If it does not, cook another 2 to 4 minutes.
9. Remove the tenders and let cool 5 minutes before serving. Repeat until all the tenders are cooked.

Mediterranean Stuffed Chicken Breasts

Servings: 4

Cooking Time: 24 Minutes

Ingredients:

- 4 boneless, skinless chicken breasts
- ½ teaspoon salt
- ½ teaspoon black pepper
- ½ teaspoon garlic powder
- ½ teaspoon paprika
- ½ cup canned artichoke hearts, chopped
- 4 ounces cream cheese
- ¼ cup grated Parmesan cheese

Directions:

1. Pat the chicken breasts with a paper towel. Using a sharp knife, cut a pouch in the side of each chicken breast for filling.

2. In a small bowl, mix the salt, pepper, garlic powder, and paprika. Season the chicken breasts with this mixture.

3. In a medium bowl, mix together the artichokes, cream cheese, and grated Parmesan cheese. Divide the filling between the 4 breasts, stuffing it inside the pouches. Use toothpicks to close the pouches and secure the filling.

4. Preheat the toaster oven to 360°F.

5. Spray the air fryer oven liberally with cooking spray, add the stuffed chicken breasts to the air fryer oven, and spray liberally with cooking spray again. Air-fry for 14 minutes, carefully turn over the chicken breasts, and cook another 10 minutes. Check the temperature at 20 minutes cooking. Chicken breasts are fully cooked when the center measures 165°F. Cook in batches, if needed.

Chicken Cordon Bleu

Servings: 4
Cooking Time: 25 Minutes

Ingredients:
- Oil spray (hand-pumped)
- 4 (4-ounce) chicken breasts
- 4 teaspoons Dijon mustard
- 4 slices Gruyère cheese
- 4 slices lean ham
- 1 cup all-purpose flour
- 2 large eggs
- 1 cup bread crumbs
- ½ cup Parmesan cheese

Directions:
1. Preheat the toaster oven to 350°F on AIR FRY for 5 minutes.
2. Place the air-fryer basket in the baking tray and generously spray it with the oil.
3. Place a chicken breast flat on a clean work surface and cut along the length of the breast, almost in half, holding the knife parallel to the counter. Open the breast up like a book and place it between two pieces of plastic wrap. Pound the chicken breast to about ¼-inch thick with a rolling pin or mallet. Repeat with the remaining breasts.
4. Spread the mustard on each breast, place a piece of cheese and ham in the center, and fold the sides of the breast over the cheese and ham. Roll the breast up from the unfolded sides to form a sealed packet. Secure with a toothpick.
5. Repeat with the remaining breasts.
6. Sprinkle the flour on a plate and set it on your work surface.
7. In a small bowl, whisk the eggs until well beaten and place next to the flour.
8. In a medium bowl, stir the bread crumbs and Parmesan and place next to the eggs.
9. Dredge the chicken rolls in the flour, then egg, then the bread crumb mixture, making sure they are completely breaded.
10. Arrange the chicken in the basket and spray lightly all over with the oil.
11. In position 2, air fry for 25 minutes, turning halfway through, until golden brown. Serve.

Jerk Turkey Meatballs

Servings: 7

Cooking Time: 8 Minutes

Ingredients:

- 1 pound lean ground turkey
- ¼ cup chopped onion
- 1 teaspoon minced garlic
- ½ teaspoon dried thyme
- ¼ teaspoon ground cinnamon
- 1 teaspoon cayenne pepper
- ½ teaspoon paprika
- ½ teaspoon salt
- ⅛ teaspoon black pepper
- ¼ teaspoon red pepper flakes
- 2 teaspoons brown sugar
- 1 large egg, whisked
- ⅓ cup panko breadcrumbs
- 2⅓ cups cooked brown Jasmine rice
- 2 green onions, chopped
- ¾ cup sweet onion dressing

Directions:

1. Preheat the toaster oven to 350°F.
2. In a medium bowl, mix the ground turkey with the onion, garlic, thyme, cinnamon, cayenne pepper, paprika, salt, pepper, red pepper flakes, and brown sugar. Add the whisked egg and stir in the breadcrumbs until the turkey starts to hold together.
3. Using a 1-ounce scoop, portion the turkey into meatballs. You should get about 28 meatballs.
4. Spray the air fryer oven with olive oil spray.
5. Place the meatballs into the air fryer oven and air-fry for 5 minutes, rotate the meatball, and cook another 2 to 4 minutes (or until the internal temperature of the meatballs reaches 165°F).
6. Remove the meatballs from the air fryer oven and repeat for the remaining meatballs.
7. Serve warm over a bed of rice with chopped green onions and spicy Caribbean jerk dressing.

Fiesta Chicken Plate

Servings: 4
Cooking Time: 15 Minutes

Ingredients:

- 1 pound boneless, skinless chicken breasts (2 large breasts)
- 2 tablespoons lime juice
- 1 teaspoon cumin
- ½ teaspoon salt
- ½ cup grated Pepper Jack cheese
- 1 16-ounce can refried beans
- ½ cup salsa
- 2 cups shredded lettuce
- 1 medium tomato, chopped
- 2 avocados, peeled and sliced
- 1 small onion, sliced into thin rings
- sour cream
- tortilla chips (optional)

Directions:

1. Split each chicken breast in half lengthwise.
2. Mix lime juice, cumin, and salt together and brush on all surfaces of chicken breasts.
3. Place in air fryer oven and air-fry at 390°F for 15 minutes, until well done.
4. Divide the cheese evenly over chicken breasts and air-fry for an additional minute to melt cheese.
5. While chicken is cooking, heat refried beans on stovetop or in microwave.
6. When ready to serve, divide beans among 4 plates. Place chicken breasts on top of beans and spoon salsa over. Arrange the lettuce, tomatoes, and avocados artfully on each plate and scatter with the onion rings.
7. Pass sour cream at the table and serve with tortilla chips if desired.

Oven-crisped Chicken

Servings: 4
Cooking Time: 35 Minutes

Ingredients:

- Coating mixture:
- 1 cup cornmeal
- ¼ cup wheat germ
- 1 teaspoon paprika
- 1 teaspoon garlic powder
- Salt and butcher's pepper to taste
- 3 tablespoons olive oil
- 1 tablespoon spicy brown mustard
- 6 skinless, boneless chicken thighs

Directions:

1. Preheat the toaster oven to 375° F.
2. Combine the coating mixture ingredients in a small bowl and transfer to a plate, spreading the mixture evenly over the plate's surface. Set aside.
3. Whisk together the oil and mustard in a bowl. Add the chicken pieces and toss to coat thoroughly. Press both sides of each piece into the coating mixture to coat well. Chill in the refrigerator for 10 minutes. Transfer the chicken pieces to a broiling rack with a pan underneath.
4. BAKE, uncovered, for 35 minutes, or until the meat is tender and the coating is crisp and golden brown or browned to your preference.

Crispy Fried Onion Chicken Breasts

Servings: 2

Cooking Time: 13 Minutes

Ingredients:

- ¼ cup all-purpose flour
- salt and freshly ground black pepper
- 1 egg
- 2 tablespoons Dijon mustard
- 1½ cups crispy fried onions (like French's®)
- ½ teaspoon paprika
- 2 (5-ounce) boneless, skinless chicken breasts
- vegetable or olive oil, in a spray bottle

Directions:

1. Preheat the toaster oven to 380°F.
2. Set up a dredging station with three shallow dishes. Place the flour in the first shallow dish and season well with salt and freshly ground black pepper. Combine the egg and Dijon mustard in a second shallow dish and whisk until smooth. Place the fried onions in a sealed bag and using a rolling pin, crush them into coarse crumbs. Combine these crumbs with the paprika in the third shallow dish.
3. Dredge the chicken breasts in the flour. Shake off any excess flour and dip them into the egg mixture. Let any excess egg drip off. Then coat both sides of the chicken breasts with the crispy onions. Press the crumbs onto the chicken breasts with your hands to make sure they are well adhered.
4. Spray or brush the bottom of the air fryer oven with oil. Transfer the chicken breasts to the air fryer oven and air-fry at 380°F for 13 minutes, turning the chicken over halfway through the cooking time.
5. Serve immediately.

Air-fried Turkey Breast With Cherry Glaze

Servings: 6
Cooking Time: 54 Minutes

Ingredients:
- 1 (5-pound) turkey breast
- 2 teaspoons olive oil
- 1 teaspoon dried thyme
- ½ teaspoon dried sage
- 1 teaspoon salt
- ½ teaspoon freshly ground black pepper
- ½ cup cherry preserves
- 1 tablespoon chopped fresh thyme leaves
- 1 teaspoon soy sauce
- freshly ground black pepper

Directions:
1. All turkeys are built differently, so depending on the turkey breast and how your butcher has prepared it, you may need to trim the bottom of the ribs in order to get the turkey to sit upright in the air fryer oven without touching the heating element. The key to this recipe is getting the right size turkey breast. Once you've managed that, the rest is easy, so make sure your turkey breast fits into the air fryer oven before you Preheat the toaster oven oven.
2. Preheat the toaster oven to 350°F.
3. Brush the turkey breast all over with the olive oil. Combine the thyme, sage, salt and pepper and rub the outside of the turkey breast with the spice mixture.
4. Transfer the seasoned turkey breast to the air fryer oven, breast side up, and air-fry at 350°F for 25 minutes. Turn the turkey breast on its side and air-fry for another 12 minutes. Turn the turkey breast on the opposite side and air-fry for 12 more minutes. The internal temperature of the turkey breast should reach 165°F when fully cooked.
5. While the turkey is air-frying, make the glaze by combining the cherry preserves, fresh thyme, soy sauce and pepper in a small bowl. When the cooking time is up, return the turkey breast to an upright position and brush the glaze all over the turkey. Air-fry for a final 5 minutes, until the skin is nicely browned and crispy. Let the turkey rest, loosely tented with foil, for at least 5 minutes before slicing and serving.

SNACKS APPETIZERS AND SIDES

Crispy Ravioli Bites

Servings: 5

Cooking Time: 7 Minutes

Ingredients:

- ⅓ cup All-purpose flour
- 1 Large egg(s), well beaten
- ⅔ cup Seasoned Italian-style dried bread crumbs
- 10 ounces (about 20) Frozen mini ravioli, meat or cheese, thawed
- Olive oil spray

Directions:

1. Preheat the toaster oven to 400°F.

2. Pour the flour into a medium bowl. Set up and fill two shallow soup plates or small pie plates on your counter: one with the beaten egg(s) and one with the bread crumbs.

3. Pour all the ravioli into the flour and toss well to coat. Pick up 1 ravioli, gently shake off any excess flour, and dip the ravioli in the egg(s), coating both sides. Let any excess egg slip back into the rest, then set the ravioli in the bread crumbs, turning it several times until lightly and evenly coated on all sides. Set aside on a cutting board and continue on with the remaining ravioli.

4. Lightly coat the ravioli on both sides with olive oil spray, then set them in the air fryer oven in as close to a single layer as you can. Some can lean up against the side of the air fryer oven. Air-fry for 7 minutes, tossing the air fryer oven at the 4-minute mark to rearrange the pieces, until brown and crisp.

5. Pour the contents of the air fryer oven onto a wire rack. Cool for 5 minutes before serving.

Savory Sausage Balls

Servings: 10

Cooking Time: 8 Minutes

Ingredients:

- 2 cups all-purpose flour
- 1 tablespoon baking powder
- ½ teaspoon garlic powder
- ¼ teaspoon onion powder
- ½ teaspoon salt
- 3 tablespoons milk
- 2½ cups grated pepper jack cheese
- 1 pound fresh sausage, casing removed

Directions:

1. Preheat the toaster oven to 370°F.

2. In a large bowl, whisk together the flour, baking powder, garlic powder, onion powder, and salt. Add in the milk, grated cheese, and sausage.

3. Using a tablespoon, scoop out the sausage and roll it between your hands to form a rounded ball. You should end up with approximately 32 balls. Place them in the air fryer oven in a single layer and working in batches as necessary.

4. Air-fry for 8 minutes, or until the outer coating turns light brown.

5. Carefully remove, repeating with the remaining sausage balls.

Garlic Breadsticks

Servings: 12

Cooking Time: 7 Minutes

Ingredients:

- 1½ tablespoons Olive oil
- 1½ teaspoons Minced garlic
- ¼ teaspoon Table salt
- ¼ teaspoon Ground black pepper
- 6 ounces Purchased pizza dough (vegan dough, if that's a concern)

Directions:

1. Preheat the toaster oven to 400°F. Mix the oil, garlic, salt, and pepper in a small bowl.

2. Divide the pizza dough into 4 balls for a small air fryer oven, 6 for a medium machine, or 8 for a large, each ball about the size of a walnut in its shell. (Each should weigh 1 ounce, if you want to drag out a scale and get obsessive.) Roll each ball into a 5-inch-long stick under your clean palms on a clean, dry work surface. Brush the sticks with the oil mixture.

3. When the machine is at temperature, place the prepared dough sticks in the air fryer oven, leaving a 1-inch space between them. Air-fry undisturbed for 7 minutes, or until puffed, golden, and set to the touch.

4. Use kitchen tongs to gently transfer the breadsticks to a wire rack and repeat step 3 with the remaining dough sticks.

Creamy Parmesan Polenta

Servings: 4

Cooking Time: 60 Minutes

Ingredients:

- 2½ cups boiling water, divided, plus extra as needed
- ½ cup coarse-ground cornmeal
- ½ teaspoon table salt
- Pinch baking soda
- 1 ounce Parmesan cheese, grated (½ cup)
- 1 tablespoon unsalted butter

Directions:

1. Adjust toaster oven rack to middle position and preheat the toaster oven to 325 degrees. Combine 2 cups boiling water, cornmeal, salt, and baking soda in greased 8-inch square baking dish or pan. Transfer dish to oven and bake until water is absorbed and polenta is thickened, 35 to 40 minutes, rotating dish halfway through baking.

2. Remove baking dish from oven. Stir in remaining ½ cup boiling water, then stir in Parmesan and butter until polenta is smooth and creamy. Adjust consistency with extra boiling water as needed. Serve.

Rosemary-roasted Potatoes

Servings:4

Cooking Time: 40 Minutes

Ingredients:

- 1 pound russet potatoes, or baby potatoes, cut into 1-inch chunks
- 2 tablespoons olive oil
- 1 teaspoon garlic powder
- 1 teaspoon dried rosemary
- Sea salt, for seasoning
- Freshly ground black pepper, for seasoning

Directions:

1. Preheat the toaster oven on AIR FRY to 400°F for 5 minutes.

2. In a large bowl, toss the potatoes with the oil, garlic powder, and rosemary. Season with salt and pepper.

3. Place the air-fryer basket in the baking tray and spread the potatoes in a single layer in the basket. You may have to do two batches. Cover the first batch loosely with foil to keep it warm while you cook the second batch.

4. In position 2, AIR FRY on 400°F for 20 minutes, shaking the basket at 10 minutes, until the potatoes are tender and golden brown. Repeat with the remaining potatoes and serve.

Homemade Pretzel Bites

Servings: 8

Cooking Time: 6 Minutes

Ingredients:

- 4¾ cups filtered water, divided
- 1 tablespoon butter
- 1 package fast-rising yeast
- ½ teaspoon salt
- 2⅓ cups bread flour
- 2 tablespoons baking soda
- 2 egg whites
- 1 teaspoon kosher salt

Directions:

1. Preheat the toaster oven to 370°F.
2. In a large microwave-safe bowl, add ¾ cup of the water. Heat for 40 seconds in the microwave. Remove and whisk in the butter; then mix in the yeast and salt. Let sit 5 minutes.
3. Using a stand mixer with a dough hook attachment, add the yeast liquid and mix in the bread flour ⅓ cup at a time until all the flour is added and a dough is formed.
4. Remove the bowl from the stand; then let the dough rise 1 hour in a warm space, covered with a kitchen towel.
5. After the dough has doubled in size, remove from the bowl and punch down a few times on a lightly floured flat surface.
6. Divide the dough into 4 balls; then roll each ball out into a long, skinny, sticklike shape. Using a sharp knife, cut each dough stick into 6 pieces.
7. Repeat Step 6 for the remaining dough balls until you have about 24 bites formed.
8. Heat the remaining 4 cups of water over the stovetop in a medium pot with the baking soda stirred in.
9. Drop the pretzel bite dough into the hot water and let boil for 60 seconds, remove, and let slightly cool.
10. Lightly brush the top of each bite with the egg whites, and then cover with a pinch of kosher salt.
11. Spray the air fryer oven with olive oil spray and place the pretzel bites on top. Air-fry for 6 to 8 minutes, or until lightly browned. Remove and keep warm.
12. Repeat until all pretzel bites are cooked.
13. Serve warm.

Hot Mexican Bean Dip

Servings: 8-10

Cooking Time: 15 Minutes

Ingredients:

- 2 cans (15 oz. each) black beans, well-drained
- 8 oz. Monterey Jack cheese or Cheddar cheese, shredded
- 1/2 cup sour cream
- 1/2 cup salsa
- 1 teaspoon hot pepper sauce

Directions:

1. Preheat the toaster oven to 350°F.
2. Place black beans, half of the cheese, sour cream, salsa and hot pepper sauce in food processor bowl. Process until slightly chunky.
3. Spoon into shallow 1-quart casserole dish.
4. Sprinkle remaining cheese on top.
5. Bake 15 minutes or until bubbly.
6. Top with additional cheese, salsa and sour cream, if desired. Serve with tortilla chips.

Crispy Tofu Bites

Servings: 4

Cooking Time: 20 Minutes

Ingredients:

- 1 pound Extra firm unflavored tofu
- Vegetable oil spray

Directions:

1. Wrap the piece of tofu in a triple layer of paper towels. Place it on a wooden cutting board and set a large pot on top of it to press out excess moisture. Set aside for 10 minutes.
2. Preheat the toaster oven to 400°F.
3. Remove the pot and unwrap the tofu. Cut it into 1-inch cubes. Place these in a bowl and coat them generously with vegetable oil spray. Toss gently, then spray generously again before tossing, until all are glistening.
4. Gently pour the tofu pieces into the air fryer oven, spread them into as close to one layer as possible, and air-fry for 20 minutes, using kitchen tongs to gently rearrange the pieces at the 7- and 14-minute marks, until light brown and crisp.
5. Gently pour the tofu pieces onto a wire rack. Cool for 5 minutes before serving warm.

Avocado Fries

Servings: 8

Cooking Time: 8 Minutes

Ingredients:

- 2 medium avocados, firm but ripe
- 1 large egg
- ½ teaspoon garlic powder
- ¼ teaspoon cayenne pepper
- ¼ teaspoon salt
- ¾ cup almond flour
- ½ cup finely grated Parmesan cheese
- ½ cup gluten-free breadcrumbs

Directions:

1. Preheat the toaster oven to 370°F.
2. Rinse the outside of the avocado with water. Slice the avocado in half, slice it in half again, and then slice it in half once more to get 8 slices. Remove the outer skin. Repeat for the other avocado. Set the avocado slices aside.
3. In a small bowl, whisk the egg, garlic powder, cayenne pepper, and salt in a small bowl. Set aside.
4. In a separate bowl, pour the almond flour.
5. In a third bowl, mix the Parmesan cheese and breadcrumbs.
6. Carefully roll the avocado slices in the almond flour, then dip them in the egg wash, and coat them in the cheese and breadcrumb topping. Repeat until all 16 fries are coated.
7. Liberally spray the air fryer oven with olive oil spray and place the avocado fries into the air fryer oven, leaving a little space around the sides between fries. Depending on the size of your air fryer oven, you may need to cook these in batches.
8. Cook fries for 8 minutes, or until the outer coating turns light brown.
9. Carefully remove, repeat with remaining slices, and then serve warm.

Veggie Cheese Bites

Servings: 4

Cooking Time: 8 Minutes

Ingredients:

- 2 cups riced vegetables
- ½ cup shredded zucchini
- ½ teaspoon garlic powder
- ¼ teaspoon black pepper
- ¼ teaspoon salt
- 1 large egg
- ¾ cup shredded cheddar cheese
- ⅓ cup whole-wheat flour

Directions:

1. Preheat the toaster oven to 350°F.
2. In a large bowl, mix together the riced vegetables, zucchini, garlic powder, pepper, and salt. Mix in the egg. Stir in the shredded cheese and whole-wheat flour until a thick, doughlike consistency forms. If you need to, add 1 teaspoon of flour at a time so you can mold the batter into balls.
3. Using a 1-inch scoop, portion the batter out into about 12 balls.
4. Liberally spray the air fryer oven with olive oil spray. Then place the veggie bites inside. Leave enough room between each bite so the air can flow around them.
5. Air-fry for 8 minutes, or until the outside is slightly browned. Depending on the size of your air fryer oven, you may need to cook these in batches.
6. Remove and let cool slightly before serving.

Fried Mozzarella Sticks

Servings: 7

Cooking Time: 5 Minutes

Ingredients:

- 7 1-ounce string cheese sticks, unwrapped
- ½ cup All-purpose flour or tapioca flour
- 2 Large egg(s), well beaten
- 2¼ cups Seasoned Italian-style dried bread crumbs (gluten-free, if a concern)
- Olive oil spray

Directions:

1. Unwrap the string cheese and place the pieces in the freezer for 20 minutes (but not longer, or they will be too frozen to soften in the time given in the air fryer oven).

2. Preheat the toaster oven to 400°F.

3. Set up and fill three shallow soup plates or small pie plates on your counter: one for the flour, one for the egg(s), and one for the bread crumbs.

4. Dip a piece of cold string cheese in the flour until well coated (keep the others in the freezer). Gently tap off any excess flour, then set the stick in the egg(s). Roll it around to coat, let any excess egg mixture slip back into the rest, and set the stick in the bread crumbs. Gently roll it around to coat it evenly, even the ends. Now dip it back in the egg(s), then again in the bread crumbs, rolling it to coat well and evenly. Set the stick aside on a cutting board and coat the remaining pieces of string cheese in the same way.

5. Lightly coat the sticks all over with olive oil spray. Place them in the air fryer oven in one layer and air-fry undisturbed for 5 minutes, or until golden brown and crisp.

6. Remove from the machine and cool for 5 minutes. Use a nonstick-safe spatula to transfer the mozzarella sticks to a serving platter. Serve hot.

Sweet Potato Casserole

Servings: 4
Cooking Time: 90 Minutes

Ingredients:

- 2 tablespoons packed brown sugar, divided
- ½ teaspoon grated orange zest, divided, plus 1 tablespoon juice
- 1½ pounds sweet potatoes, peeled and cut into 1½-inch pieces
- 2 tablespoons unsalted butter, cut into 4 pieces
- 2 tablespoons heavy cream
- ½ teaspoon table salt
- ¼ teaspoon ground cinnamon
- ⅛ teaspoon pepper
- Pinch cayenne pepper

Directions:

1. Adjust toaster oven rack to middle position and preheat the toaster oven to 400 degrees. Mix 4 teaspoons sugar and ¼ teaspoon orange zest in small bowl until thoroughly combined; set aside.
2. Toss sweet potatoes and remaining 2 teaspoons sugar together in bowl, then spread into even layer on aluminum foil–lined small rimmed baking sheet. Cover sheet tightly with foil and roast until sweet potatoes are tender, 45 to 60 minutes, rotating sheet halfway through roasting. Remove sheet from oven, select broiler function, and heat broiler.
3. Transfer potatoes and any accumulated liquid to food processor. Add butter, cream, salt, cinnamon, pepper, cayenne, remaining ¼ teaspoon orange zest, and orange juice and process until completely smooth, 30 to 60 seconds, scraping down sides of bowl as needed.
4. Transfer potato puree to 8-inch square broiler-safe baking dish or pan and sprinkle evenly with reserved sugar-zest mixture. Broil sweet potatoes until topping is melted and beginning to caramelize, 10 to 12 minutes. Transfer dish to wire rack and let cool for 10 minutes. Serve.

Crispy Spiced Chickpeas

Servings: 4
Cooking Time: 12 Minutes

Ingredients:

- 1 (15 ounce) can chickpeas, drained, rinsed, and patted dry
- 1 tablespoon olive oil
- ½ teaspoon cumin
- ¼ teaspoon paprika
- ½ teaspoon ground fennel seeds
- ⅛ teaspoon cayenne pepper

Directions:

1. Combine all ingredients in a large bowl and stir to combine.
2. Preheat the toaster oven to 430°F.
3. Place chickpeas on the food tray, then insert the tray at mid position in the preheated oven.
4. Select the Air Fry function, adjust time to 12 minutes, and press Start/Pause.
5. Remove when chickpeas are crispy and golden.

Broiled Maryland Crabcakes With Creamy Herb Sauce

Servings: 8-9

Cooking Time: 8 Minutes

Ingredients:

- 1 large egg
- 3 Tablespoons mayonnaise
- 1 Tablespoon brown mustard
- 1 Tablespoon all-purpose flour
- 1 teaspoon seafood seasoning
- 1/2 teasoon salt
- 1/4 teaspoon ground black pepper
- 1 pound lump crabmeat
- 1/4 cup chopped parsley
- 1 small shallot, minced
- 1 garlic clove, minced
- Creamy Herb Sauce

Directions:

1. In a medium bowl, mix egg, mayonnaise, mustard, flour, seafood seasoning, salt and pepper until well blended.
2. Stir in crabmeat, parsley, shallots and garlic until crab is coated with mayonnaise mixture.
3. Place 1/4 cup crab mixture on broiler pan; lightly press down. Repeat with remaining mixture.
4. Set toaster oven on BROIL. Broil crabcakes 8 minutes, without turning.
5. Serve with Creamy Herb Sauce.

Stuffed Mushrooms

Servings: 10

Cooking Time: 8 Minutes

Ingredients:

- 8 ounces white mushroom caps, stems removed
- salt
- 6 fresh mozzarella cheese balls
- ground dried thyme
- ¼ roasted red pepper cut into small pieces (about ½ inch)

Directions:

1. Sprinkle inside of mushroom caps with salt to taste.
2. Cut mozzarella balls in half.
3. Stuff each cap with half a mozzarella cheese ball. Sprinkle very lightly with thyme.
4. Top each mushroom with a small strip of roasted red pepper, lightly pressing it into the cheese.
5. Air-fry at 390°F for 8 minutes or longer if you prefer softer mushrooms.

Crispy Chili Kale Chips

Servings: 4
Cooking Time: 10 Minutes

Ingredients:

- 2 cups kale, stemmed and torn into 2-inch pieces
- 1 tablespoon extra-virgin olive oil
- ½ teaspoon chipotle chili powder
- Sea salt, for seasoning

Directions:

1. Preheat the toaster oven to 350°F on AIR FRY for 5 minutes.
2. Dry the kale with paper towels. Transfer the kale to a medium bowl and add the olive oil and chili powder. Toss the kale using your hands to evenly coat the leaves with the oil.
3. Place the air-fryer basket in the baking sheet and spread the kale in a single layer in the basket. You might have to cook two batches.
4. Air fry in position 2 for 5 minutes, until the leaves are crispy.
5. Transfer the kale chips to a large bowl and repeat with the remaining kale. Season the chips with salt and serve immediately.

Breaded Zucchini

Servings: 4
Cooking Time: 10 Minutes

Ingredients:

- 1 cup all-purpose flour
- 2 large eggs
- 1½ cups panko bread crumbs
- ½ cup grated Parmesan cheese
- Sea salt, for seasoning
- Freshly ground black pepper, for seasoning
- Oil spray (hand-pumped)
- 2 zucchini, cut into ¼-inch slices

Directions:

1. Preheat the toaster oven on AIR FRY to 350°F for 5 minutes.
2. Sprinkle the flour onto a plate.
3. In a small bowl, beat the eggs and place the bowl next to the flour.
4. In a medium bowl, stir the bread crumbs and cheese and season the mixture with salt and pepper. Place the bowl next to the eggs.
5. Place the air-fryer basket on the baking sheet and generously spray the rack with oil.
6. Dredge a zucchini slice in the flour, then the eggs, then the bread crumb mixture until well coated. Place the slice in the basket and repeat with the remaining zucchini slices. Spray the slices on both sides with oil.
7. In position 2, air fry for 10 minutes, turning once at 5 minutes, until golden brown and crispy. Serve immediately.

Sweet Apple Fries

Servings: 3

Cooking Time: 8 Minutes

Ingredients:

- 2 Medium-size sweet apple(s), such as Gala or Fuji
- 1 Large egg white(s)
- 2 tablespoons Water
- 1½ cups Finely ground gingersnap crumbs (gluten-free, if a concern)
- Vegetable oil spray

Directions:

1. Preheat the toaster oven to 375°F .
2. Peel and core an apple, then cut it into 12 slices . Repeat with more apples as necessary.
3. Whisk the egg white(s) and water in a medium bowl until foamy. Add the apple slices and toss well to coat.
4. Spread the gingersnap crumbs across a dinner plate. Using clean hands, pick up an apple slice, let any excess egg white mixture slip back into the rest, and dredge the slice in the crumbs, coating it lightly but evenly on all sides. Set it aside and continue coating the remaining apple slices.
5. Lightly coat the slices on all sides with vegetable oil spray, then set them curved side down in the air fryer oven in one layer. Air-fry undisturbed for 6 minutes, or until browned and crisp. You may need to air-fry the slices for 2 minutes longer if the temperature is at 360°F.
6. Use kitchen tongs to transfer the slices to a wire rack. Cool for 2 to 3 minutes before serving.

Bacon Corn Muffins

Servings: 6

Cooking Time: 17 Minutes

Ingredients:

- 1 1/4 cups self rising cornmeal mix
- 3/4 cup buttermilk
- 1/3 cup chopped cooked bacon
- 1/4 cup butter, melted
- 1 large egg, slightly beaten

Directions:

1. Preheat toaster oven to 425°F on CONVECTION setting.
2. Stir cornmeal mix, buttermilk, bacon, butter and egg until blended.
3. Spoon batter into lightly greased muffin pan, filling 3/4 full.
4. Bake 15 to 17 minutes until toothpick inserted in center comes out clean.
5. Cool 10 minutes on wire rack; remove.

VEGETABLES AND VEGETARIAN

Rosemary New Potatoes

Servings: 4

Cooking Time: 6 Minutes

Ingredients:

- 3 large red potatoes (enough to make 3 cups sliced)
- ¼ teaspoon ground rosemary
- ¼ teaspoon ground thyme
- ⅛ teaspoon salt
- ⅛ teaspoon ground black pepper
- 2 teaspoons extra-light olive oil

Directions:

1. Preheat the toaster oven to 330°F.
2. Place potatoes in large bowl and sprinkle with rosemary, thyme, salt, and pepper.
3. Stir with a spoon to distribute seasonings evenly.
4. Add oil to potatoes and stir again to coat well.
5. Air-fry at 330°F for 4 minutes. Stir and break apart any that have stuck together.
6. Cook an additional 2 minutes or until fork-tender.

Roasted Ratatouille Vegetables

Servings: 15

Cooking Time: 2 Minutes

Ingredients:

- 1 baby or Japanese eggplant, cut into 1½-inch cubes
- 1 red pepper, cut into 1-inch chunks
- 1 yellow pepper, cut into 1-inch chunks
- 1 zucchini, cut into 1-inch chunks
- 1 clove garlic, minced
- ½ teaspoon dried basil
- 1 tablespoon olive oil
- salt and freshly ground black pepper
- ¼ cup sliced sun-dried tomatoes in oil
- 2 tablespoons chopped fresh basil

Directions:

1. Preheat the toaster oven to 400°F.
2. Toss the eggplant, peppers and zucchini with the garlic, dried basil, olive oil, salt and freshly ground black pepper.
3. Air-fry the vegetables at 400°F for 15 minutes.
4. As soon as the vegetables are tender, toss them with the sliced sun-dried tomatoes and fresh basil and serve.

Green Beans

Servings: 4

Cooking Time: 12 Minutes

Ingredients:

- 1 pound fresh green beans
- 2 tablespoons Italian salad dressing
- salt and pepper

Directions:

1. Wash beans and snap off stem ends.
2. In a large bowl, toss beans with Italian dressing.
3. Air-fry at 330°F for 5 minutes. Stir and cook 5 minutes longer. If needed, continue cooking for 2 minutes, until as tender as you like. Beans should shrivel slightly and brown in places.
4. Sprinkle with salt and pepper to taste.

Yogurt Zucchini With Onion

Servings: 4

Cooking Time: 30 Minutes

Ingredients:

- ½ cup plain fat-free yogurt
- 1 tablespoon unbleached flour
- 4 small zucchini, scrubbed and sliced into ½-inch strips
- 3 tablespoons minced fresh onion
- 1 tablespoon olive oil
- 3 tablespoons pine nuts, ground in a blender
- Salt and freshly ground black pepper

Directions:

1. Preheat the toaster oven to 400° F.
2. Whisk together the yogurt and flour in a small bowl until smooth. Transfer to a 1-quart 8½ × 8½ × 4-inch ovenproof baking dish. Add all the remaining ingredients, mixing well. Adjust the seasonings to taste. Cover the dish with aluminum foil.
3. BAKE, covered, for 25 minutes, or until the zucchini is tender. Uncover and toss gently to blend.
4. BROIL for 5 minutes, or until the top is lightly browned.

Crispy, Cheesy Leeks

Servings: 4

Cooking Time: 15 Minutes

Ingredients:

- 2 Medium leek(s), about 9 ounces each
- Olive oil spray
- ¼ cup Seasoned Italian-style dried bread crumbs (gluten-free, if a concern)
- ¼ cup (about ¾ ounce) Finely grated Parmesan cheese
- 2 tablespoons Olive oil

Directions:

1. Preheat the toaster oven to 350°F.

2. Trim off the root end of the leek(s) as well as the dark green top(s), leaving about a 5-inch usable section. Split the leek section(s) in half lengthwise. Set the leek halves cut side up on your work surface. Pull out and remove in one piece the semicircles that make up the inner structure of the leek, about halfway down. Set the removed "inside" next to the outer leek "shells" on your cutting board. Generously coat them all on all sides (particularly the "bottoms") with olive oil spray.

3. Set the leeks and their insides cut side up in the air fryer oven with as much air space between them as possible. Air-fry undisturbed for 12 minutes.

4. Meanwhile, mix the bread crumbs, cheese, and olive oil in a small bowl until well combined.

5. After 12 minutes in the air fryer oven, sprinkle this mixture inside the leek shells and on top of the leek insides. Increase the machine's temperature to 375°F (or 380°F or 390°F, if one of these is the closest setting). Air-fry undisturbed for 3 minutes, or until the topping is lightly browned.

6. Use a nonstick-safe spatula to transfer the leeks to a serving platter. Cool for a few minutes before serving warm.

Honey-roasted Parsnips

Servings: 3

Cooking Time: 23 Minutes

Ingredients:

- 1½ pounds Medium parsnips, peeled
- Olive oil spray
- 1 tablespoon Honey
- 1½ teaspoons Water
- ¼ teaspoon Table salt

Directions:

1. Preheat the toaster oven to 350°F .

2. If the thick end of a parsnip is more than ½ inch in diameter, cut the parsnip just below where it swells to its large end, then slice the large section in half lengthwise. Generously coat the parsnips on all sides with olive oil spray.

3. When the machine is at temperature, set the parsnips in the air fryer oven with as much air space between them as possible. Air-fry undisturbed for 20 minutes.

4. Whisk the honey, water, and salt in a small bowl until smooth. Brush this mixture over the parsnips. Air-fry undisturbed for 3 minutes more, or until the glaze is lightly browned.

5. Use kitchen tongs to transfer the parsnips to a wire rack or a serving platter. Cool for a couple of minutes before serving.

Fried Eggplant Slices

Servings: 3

Cooking Time: 12 Minutes

Ingredients:

- 1½ sleeves (about 60 saltines) Saltine crackers
- ¾ cup Cornstarch
- 2 Large egg(s), well beaten
- 1 medium (about ¾ pound) Eggplant, stemmed, peeled, and cut into ¼-inch-thick rounds
- Olive oil spray

Directions:

1. Preheat the toaster oven to 400°F. Also, position the rack in the center of the oven and heat the oven to 175°F.

2. Grind the saltines, in batches if necessary, in a food processor, pulsing the machine and rearranging the saltine pieces every few pulses. Or pulverize the saltines in a large, heavy zip-closed plastic bag with the bottom of a heavy saucepan. In either case, you want small bits of saltines, not just crumbs.

3. Set up and fill three shallow soup plates or small pie plates on your counter: one for the cornstarch, one for the beaten egg(s), and one for the pulverized saltines.

4. Set an eggplant slice in the cornstarch and turn it to coat on both sides. Use a brush to lightly remove any excess. Dip it into the beaten egg(s) and turn to coat both sides. Let any excess egg slip back into the rest, then set the slice in the saltines. Turn several times, pressing gently to coat both sides evenly but not heavily. Coat both sides of the slice with olive oil spray and set it aside. Continue dipping and coating the remaining slices.

5. Set one, two, or maybe three slices in the pan. There should be at least ½ inch between them for proper air flow. Air-fry undisturbed for 12 minutes, or until crisp and browned.

6. Use a nonstick-safe spatula to transfer the slice(s) to a large baking sheet. Slip it into the oven to keep the slices warm as you air-fry more batches, as needed, always transferring the slices to the baking sheet to stay warm.

Roasted Garlic Potatoes

Servings: 2

Cooking Time: 40 Minutes

Ingredients:

- 2 medium potatoes, peeled and chopped
- 6 garlic cloves, roasted
- 1 tablespoon olive oil
- Salt and freshly ground black pepper
- 1 tablespoon chopped fresh parsley

Directions:

1. Preheat the toaster oven to 400° F.

2. Place the potatoes in an oiled or nonstick 8½ × 8½ × 2-inch square baking (cake) pan. Add the garlic, oil, and salt and pepper to taste. Toss to coat well. Cover the pan with aluminum foil.

3. BAKE, covered, for 40 minutes, or until the potatoes are tender. Remove the cover.

4. BROIL 10 minutes, or until lightly browned. Garnish with fresh parsley before serving.

Potato Shells With Cheese And Bacon

Servings: 4

Cooking Time: 8 Minutes

Ingredients:

- 4 tablespoons shredded reduced-fat cheddar cheese
- 4 slices lean turkey bacon, cooked and crumbled
- 4 potato shells
- 4 tablespoons nonfat sour cream
- 4 teaspoons chopped fresh or frozen chives
- Salt and freshly ground black pepper

Directions:

1. Sprinkle 1 tablespoon Cheddar cheese and 1 tablespoon crumbled bacon into each potato shell. Place the shells on a broiling rack with a pan underneath.

2. BROIL for 8 minutes, or until the cheese is melted and the shells lightly browned. Spoon 1 tablespoon sour cream into each shell and sprinkle with 1 teaspoon chives. Add salt and pepper to taste.

Baked Mac And Cheese

Servings: 4

Cooking Time: 45 Minutes

Ingredients:

- Oil spray (hand-pumped)
- 1½ cups whole milk, room temperature
- ½ cup heavy (whipping) cream, room temperature
- 1 cup shredded cheddar cheese
- 4 ounces cream cheese, room temperature
- ½ teaspoon dry mustard
- ⅛ teaspoon sea salt
- ⅛ teaspoon freshly ground black pepper
- 1¼ cups dried elbow macaroni
- ¼ cup bread crumbs
- 2 tablespoons grated Parmesan cheese
- 1 tablespoon salted butter, melted

Directions:

1. Place the rack in position 1 and preheat the toaster oven to 375°F on CONVECTION BAKE for 5 minutes.

2. Lightly coat an 8-inch-square baking dish with the oil spray.

3. In a large bowl, stir the milk, cream, cheddar, cream cheese, mustard, salt, and pepper until well combined.

4. Transfer the mixture to the baking dish, stir in the macaroni and cover tightly with foil.

5. Bake for 35 minutes.

6. While the macaroni is baking, in a small bowl, stir the bread crumbs, Parmesan, and butter to form coarse crumbs. Set aside.

7. Take the baking dish out of the oven, uncover, stir, and evenly cover with the bread crumb mixture.

8. Bake uncovered for an additional 10 minutes until the pasta is tender, bubbly, and golden brown. Serve.

Crispy Noodle Salad

Servings: 3

Cooking Time: 22 Minutes

Ingredients:

- 6 ounces Fresh Chinese-style stir-fry or lo mein wheat noodles
- 1½ tablespoons Cornstarch
- ¾ cup Chopped stemmed and cored red bell pepper
- 2 Medium scallion(s), trimmed and thinly sliced
- 2 teaspoons Sambal oelek or other pulpy hot red pepper sauce
- 2 teaspoons Thai sweet chili sauce or red ketchup-like chili sauce, such as Heinz
- 2 teaspoons Regular or low-sodium soy sauce or tamari sauce
- 2 teaspoons Unseasoned rice vinegar
- 1 tablespoon White or black sesame seeds

Directions:

1. Bring a large saucepan of water to a boil over high heat. Add the noodles and boil for 2 minutes. Drain in a colander set in the sink. Rinse several times with cold water, shaking the colander to drain the noodles very well. Spread the noodles out on a large cutting board and air-dry for 10 minutes.

2. Preheat the toaster oven to 400°F.

3. Toss the noodles in a bowl with the cornstarch until well coated. Spread them out across the entire air fryer oven (although they will be touching and overlapping a bit). Air-fry for 6 minutes, then turn the solid mass of noodles over as one piece. If it cracks in half or smaller pieces, just fit these back together after turning. Continue air-frying for 6 minutes, or until golden brown and crisp.

4. As the noodles cook, stir the bell pepper, scallion(s), sambal oelek, red chili sauce, soy sauce, vinegar, and sesame seeds in a serving bowl until well combined.

5. Turn the air fryer oven of noodles out onto a cutting board and cool for a minute or two. Break the mass of noodles into individual noodles and/or small chunks and add to the dressing in the serving bowl. Toss well to serve.

Golden Grilled Cheese Tomato Sandwich

Servings: 2

Cooking Time: 10 Minutes

Ingredients:

- 4 slices whole-grain bread
- 4 teaspoons salted butter at room temperature, divided
- 4 to 6 slices cheddar cheese, or your favorite cheese
- 1 large tomato, thinly sliced

Directions:

1. Preheat the toaster oven to 350°F on AIR FRY for 5 minutes.
2. Place the air-fryer basket in the baking sheet and set aside.
3. Butter all four pieces of bread, using 1 teaspoon of butter for each and place 2 pieces of bread, butter-side down, in the basket. Evenly divide the cheese between the 2 bread slices and top with tomato slices. Place the remaining 2 pieces of bread on the tomatoes, butter-side up.
4. Place the tray in position 2 and air fry for 5 minutes until golden brown. Flip the sandwiches and air fry until the cheese is melted and the other side of the bread is golden brown, about 5 minutes. Serve.

Crispy Herbed Potatoes

Servings: 6

Cooking Time: 20 Minutes

Ingredients:

- 3 medium baking potatoes, washed and cubed
- ½ teaspoon dried thyme
- 1 teaspoon minced dried rosemary
- ½ teaspoon garlic powder
- 1 teaspoon sea salt
- ½ teaspoon black pepper
- 2 tablespoons extra-virgin olive oil
- ¼ cup chopped parsley

Directions:

1. Preheat the toaster oven to 390°F.
2. Pat the potatoes dry. In a large bowl, mix together the cubed potatoes, thyme, rosemary, garlic powder, sea salt, and pepper. Drizzle and toss with olive oil.
3. Pour the herbed potatoes into the air fryer oven. Air-fry for 20 minutes, stirring every 5 minutes.
4. Toss the cooked potatoes with chopped parsley and serve immediately.
5. VARY IT! Potatoes are versatile — add any spice or seasoning mixture you prefer and create your own favorite side dish.

Potatoes Au Gratin

Servings: 4
Cooking Time: 40 Minutes

Ingredients:

- Mixture:
- ½ cup fat-free half-and-half
- ¼ cup nonfat plain yogurt
- 2 tablespoons margarine
- 2 tablespoons unbleached flour
- 1 teaspoon garlic powder
- ¼ cup shredded low-fat mozzarella cheese
- 2 tablespoons grated Parmesan cheese
- Salt and butcher's pepper to taste
- 2 cups peeled and diced potatoes
- ½ cup chopped onion
- 1 tablespoon fresh or frozen chives
- ¼ teaspoon paprika

Directions:

1. Preheat the toaster oven to 400° F.
2. Process the mixture ingredients in a food processor or blender until smooth. Pour into a 1-quart 8½ × 8½ × 4-inch ovenproof baking dish.
3. Add the potatoes, onion, chives, and paprika and stir to mix well. Cover the dish with aluminum foil.
4. BAKE, covered, for 40 minutes, or until the potatoes and onion are tender.

Pecan Parmesan Cauliflower

Servings: 4
Cooking Time: 35 Minutes

Ingredients:

- 2½ cups (frozen thawed or fresh) thinly sliced cauliflower florets
- Salt and freshly ground black pepper
- 3 tablespoons freshly grated Parmesan cheese
- ½ cup ground pecans

Directions:

1. Preheat the toaster oven to 400° F.
2. Combine the florets and oil in a 1-quart 8½ × 8½ × 4-inch ovenproof baking dish, tossing to coat well. Season to taste with salt and pepper. Cover the dish with aluminum foil.
3. BAKE for 25 minutes, or until tender. Uncover and sprinkle with the cheese and pecans.
4. BROIL for 10 minutes, or until lightly browned.

Chilaquiles

Servings: 4
Cooking Time: 25 Minutes

Ingredients:

- Oil spray (hand-pumped)
- 1¼ cups store-bought salsa
- 1 (15-ounce) can low-sodium navy or black beans, drained and rinsed
- ½ cup corn kernels
- ¼ cup chicken broth
- ¼ sweet onion, chopped
- ½ teaspoon minced garlic
- 25 tortilla chips, broken up into 2-inch pieces
- 1½ cups queso fresco cheese, crumbled
- 1 avocado, chopped
- 1 scallion, white and green parts, chopped

Directions:

1. Place the rack in position 1 and preheat the toaster oven to 400°F on BAKE for 5 minutes.
2. Lightly coat an 8-inch-square baking dish with oil spray and set aside.
3. In a large bowl, stir the salsa, beans, corn, chicken broth, onion, and garlic until well mixed.
4. Add the tortilla chips and stir to combine. It is okay if the tortilla chips break up a little.
5. Transfer the mixture to the baking dish, top with the cheese, and cover tightly with foil.
6. Bake for 20 minutes until the chips are soft, the mixture is bubbly, and then uncover and bake until the cheese is golden and melted, about 5 minutes.
7. Serve topped with the avocado and scallion.

Broiled Tomatoes

Servings: 4
Cooking Time: 10 Minutes

Ingredients:

- 2 medium tomatoes
- Filling:
- 2 tablespoons grated Parmesan cheese
- 2 tablespoons bread crumbs
- 2 tablespoons olive oil
- 1 teaspoon dried oregano or 1 tablespoon chopped fresh oregano
- 1 teaspoon garlic powder or 2 garlic cloves, minced
- Salt and freshly ground black pepper to taste

Directions:

1. Slice the tomatoes in half through the stem scar (top) and carefully scoop out the seeds and flesh with a teaspoon. (Remove and discard about 1 tablespoon each.)
2. Mix together the filling ingredients in a small bowl and adjust the seasonings. Fill each tomato half cavity with equal portions of the mixture. Place the tomato halves in an oiled or nonstick 8½ × 8½ × 2-inch square baking (cake) pan.
3. BROIL for 10 minutes, or until the tomatoes are cooked and the tops are browned.

Zucchini Boats With Ham And Cheese

Servings: 4

Cooking Time: 12 Minutes

Ingredients:

- 2 6-inch-long zucchini
- 2 ounces Thinly sliced deli ham, any rind removed, meat roughly chopped
- 4 Dry-packed sun-dried tomatoes, chopped
- ⅓ cup Purchased pesto
- ¼ cup Packaged mini croutons
- ¼ cup (about 1 ounce) Shredded semi-firm mozzarella cheese

Directions:

1. Preheat the toaster oven to 375°F .

2. Split the zucchini in half lengthwise and use a flatware spoon or a serrated grapefruit spoon to scoop out the insides of the halves, leaving at least a ¼-inch border all around the zucchini half. (You can save the scooped out insides to add to soups and stews—or even freeze it for a much later use.)

3. Mix the ham, sun-dried tomatoes, pesto, croutons, and half the cheese in a bowl until well combined. Pack this mixture into the zucchini "shells." Top them with the remaining cheese.

4. Set them stuffing side up in the air fryer oven without touching (even a fraction of an inch between them is enough room). Air-fry undisturbed for 12 minutes, or until softened and browned, with the cheese melted on top.

5. Use a nonstick-safe spatula to transfer the zucchini boats stuffing side up on a wire rack. Cool for 5 or 10 minutes before serving.

Steakhouse Baked Potatoes

Servings: 3

Cooking Time: 55 Minutes

Ingredients:

- 3 10-ounce russet potatoes
- 2 tablespoons Olive oil
- 1 teaspoon Table salt

Directions:

1. Preheat the toaster oven to 375°F .

2. Poke holes all over each potato with a fork. Rub the skin of each potato with 2 teaspoons of the olive oil, then sprinkle ¼ teaspoon salt all over each potato.

3. When the machine is at temperature, set the potatoes in the air fryer oven in one layer with as much air space between them as possible. Air-fry for 50 minutes, turning once, or until soft to the touch but with crunchy skins. If the machine is at 360°F, you may need to add up to 5 minutes to the cooking time.

4. Use kitchen tongs to gently transfer the baked potatoes to a wire rack. Cool for 5 or 10 minutes before serving.

DESSERTS

Almond Amaretto Bundt Cake

Servings: 8

Cooking Time: 37 Minutes

Ingredients:
- Nonstick baking spray with flour
- 1 (15.25- to 18-ounce) box yellow cake mix
- 1 (3.9-ounce) box vanilla instant pudding
- 1 cup sour cream
- ½ cup canola or vegetable oil
- ¼ cup amaretto or almond liqueur
- 4 large eggs
- ¼ teaspoon pure almond extract
- GLAZE
- 2 ½ cups confectioners' sugar
- 2 tablespoons amaretto
- 1 teaspoon pure vanilla extract
- 1 to 2 tablespoons milk
- Sliced almonds, toasted

Directions:

1. Preheat the toaster oven to 350°F. Spray a 12-cup Bundt pan with nonstick baking spray with flour.

2. Beat the cake mix, instant pudding, sour cream, oil, ¼ cup water, the amaretto, eggs, and almond extract in a large bowl with a handheld mixer at low speed for 30 seconds to combine the ingredients. Scrape the sides of the bowl with a rubber scraper. Beat on medium-high speed for 2 minutes.

3. Pour the batter into the prepared pan. Bake for 30 to 35 minutes, or until a wooden pick inserted into the center comes out clean.

4. Place the pan on a wire rack to cool for 10 minutes. Invert the cake onto the rack and let cool completely.

5. Meanwhile, make the glaze: Whisk the sugar, amaretto, vanilla, and 1 tablespoon milk in a small bowl. If needed, stir in the additional milk to make the desired consistency. Pour over the cake. Garnish with the sliced almonds.

Pineapple Tartlets

Servings: 4
Cooking Time: 20 Minutes

Ingredients:

- Vegetable oil
- 6 sheets phyllo pastry
- 1 8-ounce can crushed pineapple, drained
- 3 tablespoons low-fat cottage cheese
- 2 tablespoons orange or pineapple marmalade
- 6 teaspoons concentrated thawed frozen orange juice
- Vanilla frozen yogurt or nonfat whipped topping

Directions:

1. Preheat the toaster oven to 350° F.
2. Brush the pans of a 6-muffin tin with vegetable oil. Lay a phyllo sheet on a clean, flat surface and brush with oil. Fold the sheet into quarters to fit the muffin pan. Repeat the process for the remaining phyllo sheets and pans.
3. BAKE for 5 minutes, or until lightly browned. Remove from the oven and cool.
4. Combine the pineapple, cottage cheese, and marmalade in a small bowl, mixing well. Fill the phyllo shells (in the pans) with equal portions of the mixture. Drizzle 1 teaspoon orange juice concentrate over each.
5. BAKE at 400° F. for 15 minutes, or until the filling is cooked. Cool and remove the tartlets carefully from the muffin pans to dessert dishes. Top with vanilla frozen yogurt or nonfat whipped topping.

Blueberry Cheesecake Tartlets

Servings: 9

Cooking Time: 6 Minutes

Ingredients:

- 8 ounces cream cheese, softened
- ¼ cup sugar
- 1 egg
- ½ teaspoon vanilla extract
- zest of 2 lemons, divided
- 9 mini graham cracker tartlet shells
- 2 cups blueberries
- ½ teaspoon ground cinnamon
- juice of ½ lemon
- ¼ cup apricot preserves

Directions:

1. Preheat the toaster oven to 330°F.

2. Combine the cream cheese, sugar, egg, vanilla and the zest of one lemon in a medium bowl and blend until smooth by hand or with an electric hand mixer. Pour the cream cheese mixture into the tartlet shells.

3. Air-fry 3 tartlets at a time at 330°F for 6 minutes, rotating them in the air fryer oven halfway through the cooking time.

4. Combine the blueberries, cinnamon, zest of one lemon and juice of half a lemon in a bowl. Melt the apricot preserves in the microwave or over low heat in a saucepan. Pour the apricot preserves over the blueberries and gently toss to coat.

5. Allow the cheesecakes to cool completely and then top each one with some of the blueberry mixture. Garnish the tartlets with a little sugared lemon peel and refrigerate until you are ready to serve.

Peanut Butter S'mores

Servings: 10

Cooking Time: 1 Minutes

Ingredients:

- 10 Graham crackers (full, double-square cookies as they come out of the package)
- 5 tablespoons Natural-style creamy or crunchy peanut butter
- ½ cup Milk chocolate chips
- 10 Standard-size marshmallows (not minis and not jumbo campfire ones)

Directions:

1. Preheat the toaster oven to 350°F.

2. Break the graham crackers in half widthwise at the marked place, so the rectangle is now in two squares. Set half of the squares flat side up on your work surface. Spread each with about 1½ teaspoons peanut butter, then set 10 to 12 chocolate chips point side up into the peanut butter on each, pressing gently so the chips stick.

3. Flatten a marshmallow between your clean, dry hands and set it atop the chips. Do the same with the remaining marshmallows on the other coated graham crackers. Do not set the other half of the graham crackers on top of these coated graham crackers.

4. When the machine is at temperature, set the treats graham cracker side down in a single layer in the air fryer oven. They may touch, but even a fraction of an inch between them will provide better air flow. Air-fry undisturbed for 45 seconds.

5. Use a nonstick-safe spatula to transfer the topped graham crackers to a wire rack. Set the other graham cracker squares flat side down over the marshmallows. Cool for a couple of minutes before serving.

Orange Strawberry Flan

Servings: 4

Cooking Time: 45 Minutes

Ingredients:

- ¼ cup sugar
- ½ cup concentrated orange juice
- 1 12-ounce can low-fat evaporated milk
- 3 egg yolks
- 1 cup frozen strawberries, thawed and sliced, or 1 cup fresh strawberries, washed, stemmed, and sliced
- 4 fresh mint sprigs

Directions:

1. Preheat the toaster oven to 375° F.

2. Place the sugar in a baking pan and broil for 4 minutes, or until the sugar melts. Remove from the oven, stir briefly, and pour equal portions of the caramelized sugar into four 1-cup-size ovenproof dishes. Set aside.

3. Blend the orange juice, evaporated milk, and egg yolks in a food processor or blender until smooth. Transfer the mixture to a medium bowl and fold in the sliced strawberries. Pour the mixture in equal portions into the four dishes.

4. BAKE for 45 minutes, or until a knife inserted in the center comes out clean. Chill for several hours. The flan may be loosened by running a knife around the edge and inverted on individual plates or served in the dishes. Garnish with fresh mint sprigs.

Honey-roasted Mixed Nuts

Servings: 8

Cooking Time: 15 Minutes

Ingredients:

- ½ cup raw, shelled pistachios
- ½ cup raw almonds
- 1 cup raw walnuts
- 2 tablespoons filtered water
- 2 tablespoons honey
- 1 tablespoon vegetable oil
- 2 tablespoons sugar
- ½ teaspoon salt

Directions:

1. Preheat the toaster oven to 300°F.

2. Lightly spray an air-fryer-safe pan with olive oil; then place the pistachios, almonds, and walnuts inside the pan and place the pan inside the air fryer oven.

3. Air-fry for 15 minutes, every 5 minutes to rotate the nuts.

4. While the nuts are roasting, boil the water in a small pan and stir in the honey and oil. Continue to stir while cooking until the water begins to evaporate and a thick sauce is formed. The sauce should stick to the back of a wooden spoon when mixed. Turn off the heat.

5. Remove the nuts from the air fryer oven (cooking should have just completed) and spoon the nuts into the stovetop pan. Use a spatula to coat the nuts with the honey syrup.

6. Line a baking sheet with parchment paper and spoon the nuts onto the sheet. Lightly sprinkle the sugar and salt over the nuts and let cool in the refrigerator for at least 2 hours.

7. When the honey and sugar have hardened, store the nuts in an airtight container in the refrigerator.

Donut Holes

Servings: 13
Cooking Time: 12 Minutes

Ingredients:
- 6 tablespoons Granulated white sugar
- 1½ tablespoons Butter, melted and cooled
- 2 tablespoons (or 1 small egg, well beaten) Pasteurized egg substitute, such as Egg Beaters
- 6 tablespoons Regular or low-fat sour cream (not fat-free)
- ¾ teaspoon Vanilla extract
- 1⅔ cups All-purpose flour
- ¾ teaspoon Baking powder
- ¼ teaspoon Table salt
- Vegetable oil spray

Directions:
1. Preheat the toaster oven to 350°F .
2. Whisk the sugar and melted butter in a medium bowl until well combined. Whisk in the egg substitute or egg , then the sour cream and vanilla until smooth. Remove the whisk and stir in the flour, baking powder, and salt with a wooden spoon just until a soft dough forms.
3. Use 2 tablespoons of this dough to create a ball between your clean palms. Set it aside and continue making balls: 8 more for the small batch, 12 more for the medium batch, or 17 more for the large one.
4. Coat the balls in the vegetable oil spray, then set them in the air fryer oven with as much air space between them as possible. Even a fraction of an inch will be enough, but they should not touch. Air-fry undisturbed for 12 minutes, or until browned and cooked through. A toothpick inserted into the center of a ball should come out clean.
5. Pour the contents of the air fryer oven onto a wire rack. Cool for at least 5 minutes before serving.

Spice Cake

Servings: 6

Cooking Time: 25 Minutes

Ingredients:

- 1 cup applesauce or 2 4-ounce jars baby food prunes
- ¼ cup skim milk or low-fat soy milk
- 1 tablespoon vegetable oil
- ½ cup brown sugar
- 1 egg
- 1½ cups unbleached flour
- 1 teaspoon baking powder
- ½ teaspoon baking soda
- ¼ teaspoon grated nutmeg
- ½ teaspoon ground cinnamon
- ½ teaspoon grated orange zest
- Salt to taste
- Creamy Frosting

Directions:

1. Preheat the toaster oven to 350° F.
2. Stir together the applesauce, milk, oil, sugar, and egg in a small bowl. Set aside.
3. Combine the flour, baking powder, nutmeg, cinnamon, orange zest, and salt in a medium bowl. Add the applesauce mixture and stir to mix well. Pour the batter into an oiled or nonstick 8½ × 8½ × 2-inch square baking (cake) pan.
4. BAKE for 25 minutes, or until a toothpick inserted in the center comes out clean. Frost with Creamy Frosting.

White Chocolate Cranberry Blondies

Servings: 6
Cooking Time: 18 Minutes

Ingredients:
- ⅓ cup butter
- ½ cup sugar
- 1 teaspoon vanilla extract
- 1 large egg
- 1 cup all-purpose flour
- ½ teaspoon baking powder
- ⅛ teaspoon salt
- ¼ cup dried cranberries
- ¼ cup white chocolate chips

Directions:
1. Preheat the toaster oven to 320°F.
2. In a large bowl, cream the butter with the sugar and vanilla extract. Whisk in the egg and set aside.
3. In a separate bowl, mix the flour with the baking powder and salt. Then gently mix the dry ingredients into the wet. Fold in the cranberries and chocolate chips.
4. Liberally spray an oven-safe 7-inch springform pan with olive oil and pour the batter into the pan.
5. Air-fry for 17 minutes or until a toothpick inserted in the center comes out clean.
6. Remove and let cool 5 minutes before serving.

Fried Oreos

Servings: 12
Cooking Time: 7 Minutes

Ingredients:
- 1 Large egg white(s)
- 2 tablespoons Water
- 1 cup Graham cracker crumbs
- 12 Original-size Oreos (not minis or king-size)
- Vegetable oil spray

Directions:
1. Preheat the toaster oven to 375°F .
2. Set up and fill two shallow soup plates or small pie plates on your counter: one for the egg white(s), whisked with the water until foamy; and one for the graham cracker crumbs.
3. Dip a cookie in the egg white mixture, turning several times to coat well. Let any excess egg white mixture slip back into the rest, then set the cookie in the crumbs. Turn several times to coat evenly, pressing gently. You want an even but not thick crust. However, make sure that the cookie is fully coated and that the filling is sealed inside. Lightly coat the cookie on all sides with vegetable oil spray. Set aside and continue dipping and coating the remaining cookies.
4. Set the coated cookies in the oven with as much air space between them as possible. Air-fry undisturbed for 6 minutes, or until the coating is golden brown and set. If the machine is at 360°F, the cookies may need 1 minute more to cook and set.
5. Use a nonstick-safe spatula to transfer the cookies to a wire rack. Cool for at least 5 minutes before serving.

Keto Cheesecake Cups

Servings: 6

Cooking Time: 10 Minutes

Ingredients:

- 8 ounces cream cheese
- ¼ cup plain whole-milk Greek yogurt
- 1 large egg
- 1 teaspoon pure vanilla extract
- 3 tablespoons monk fruit sweetener
- ¼ teaspoon salt
- ½ cup walnuts, roughly chopped

Directions:

1. Preheat the toaster oven to 315°F.
2. In a large bowl, use a hand mixer to beat the cream cheese together with the yogurt, egg, vanilla, sweetener, and salt. When combined, fold in the chopped walnuts.
3. Set 6 silicone muffin liners inside an air-fryer-safe pan.
4. Evenly fill the cupcake liners with cheesecake batter.
5. Carefully place the pan into the air fryer oven and air-fry for about 10 minutes, or until the tops are lightly browned and firm.
6. Carefully remove the pan when done and place in the refrigerator for 3 hours to firm up before serving.

Cheese Blintzes

Servings: 6

Cooking Time: 10 Minutes

Ingredients:

- 1½ 7½-ounce package(s) farmer cheese
- 3 tablespoons Regular or low-fat cream cheese (not fat-free)
- 3 tablespoons Granulated white sugar
- ¼ teaspoon Vanilla extract
- 6 Egg roll wrappers
- 3 tablespoons Butter, melted and cooled

Directions:

1. Preheat the toaster oven to 375°F.
2. Use a flatware fork to mash the farmer cheese, cream cheese, sugar, and vanilla in a small bowl until smooth.
3. Set one egg roll wrapper on a clean, dry work surface. Place ¼ cup of the filling at the edge closest to you, leaving a ½-inch gap before the edge of the wrapper. Dip your clean finger in water and wet the edges of the wrapper. Fold the perpendicular sides over the filling, then roll the wrapper closed with the filling inside. Set it aside seam side down and continue filling the remainder of the wrappers.
4. Brush the wrappers on all sides with the melted butter. Be generous. Set them seam side down in the air fryer oven with as much space between them as possible. Air-fry undisturbed for 10 minutes, or until lightly browned.
5. Use a nonstick-safe spatula to transfer the blintzes to a wire rack. Cool for at least 5 minutes or up to 20 minutes before serving.

Goat Cheese–stuffed Nectarines

Servings: 4

Cooking Time: 10 Minutes

Ingredients:

- 4 ripe nectarines, halved and pitted
- 1 tablespoon olive oil
- 1 cup soft goat cheese, room temperature
- 1 tablespoon maple syrup
- ¼ teaspoon vanilla extract
- ¼ teaspoon ground cinnamon
- 2 tablespoons pecans, chopped

Directions:

1. Preheat the toaster oven to 350°F on AIR FRY for 5 minutes.

2. Place the air-fryer basket in the baking tray and place the nectarines in the basket, hollow-side up. Brush the tops and hollow of the fruit with the olive oil.

3. In position 2, air fry for 5 minutes to soften and lightly brown the fruit.

4. While the fruit is air frying, in a small bowl, stir the goat cheese, maple syrup, vanilla, and cinnamon until well blended.

5. Take the fruit out and evenly divide the cheese filling between the halves. Air fry for 5 minutes until the filling is heated through and a little melted.

6. Serve topped with pecans.

Apple Strudel

Servings: 2

Cooking Time: 90 Minutes

Ingredients:

- 2 Golden Delicious apples (14 ounces), peeled, cored, and cut into ½-inch pieces
- 1½ tablespoons granulated sugar
- ¼ teaspoon grated lemon zest plus 1 teaspoon juice
- ⅛ teaspoon ground cinnamon
- ⅛ teaspoon ground ginger
- ⅛ teaspoon table salt, divided
- 2 tablespoons golden raisins
- 1 tablespoon panko bread crumbs
- 3½ tablespoons unsalted butter, melted
- 1½ teaspoons confectioners' sugar, plus extra for serving
- 7 (14 by 9-inch) phyllo sheets, thawed

Directions:

1. Toss apples, granulated sugar, lemon zest and juice, cinnamon, ginger, and pinch salt together in large bowl. Cover and microwave until apples are softened, 2 to 4 minutes, stirring once halfway through microwaving. Let apples sit, covered, for 5 minutes. Transfer apples to colander set in second large bowl and let drain, reserving liquid. Return apples to bowl; stir in raisins and panko.

2. Adjust toaster oven rack to middle position and preheat the toaster oven to 350 degrees. Spray small rimmed baking sheet with vegetable oil spray. Stir remaining pinch salt into melted butter.

3. Place 16½ by 12-inch sheet of parchment paper on counter with long side parallel to edge of counter. Place 1 phyllo sheet on parchment with long side parallel to edge of counter. Place confectioners' sugar in fine-mesh strainer. Lightly brush sheet with melted butter and dust sparingly with confectioners' sugar. Repeat with remaining 6 phyllo sheets, melted butter, and confectioners' sugar, stacking sheets one on top of other as you go.

4. Arrange apple mixture in 2½ by 10-inch rectangle 2 inches from bottom of phyllo and about 2 inches from each side. Using parchment, fold sides of phyllo over filling, then fold bottom edge of phyllo over filling. Brush folded portions of phyllo with reserved apple liquid. Fold top edge over filling, making sure top and bottom edges overlap by about 1 inch. (If they do not overlap, unfold, rearrange filling into slightly narrower strip, and refold.) Press firmly to seal. Using thin metal spatula, transfer strudel to prepared sheet. Lightly brush top and sides of strudel with remaining apple liquid.

5. Bake until golden brown, 25 to 30 minutes, rotating sheet halfway through baking. Using thin metal spatula, immediately transfer strudel to cutting board. Let cool for 3 minutes. Slice strudel and let cool for at least 20 minutes. Serve warm or at room temperature, dusting with extra confectioners' sugar before serving.

Heritage Chocolate Chip Cookies

Servings: 16-18
Cooking Time: 12 Minutes

Ingredients:

- 1 1/2 cups all-purpose flour
- 1 teaspoon baking powder
- 1/2 teaspoon salt
- 1 large egg, unbeaten
- 1/2 cup shortening
- 1/2 cup packed dark brown sugar
- 1/4 cup granulated sugar
- 2 teaspoons vanilla extract
- 1 tablespoon milk
- 1 cup chocolate chips

Directions:

1. Preheat the toaster oven to 375ºF.
2. Place all ingredients except chocolate chips in large mixer bowl. With electric mixer on low speed, beat until ingredients are mixed. Gradually increase speed to medium and beat 3 minutes, stopping to scrape bowl as needed.
3. Add chocolate chips and beat on low until blended.
4. Line cookie sheets with parchment paper. Using a small scoop, place 12 scoops of cookie dough about 1-inch apart on parchment.
5. Bake 10 to 12 minutes or until cookies are browned. Slide parchment with baked cookies onto rack to cool. Repeat with remaining dough.

Gingerbread

Servings: 6
Cooking Time: 20 Minutes

Ingredients:

- cooking spray
- 1 cup flour
- 2 tablespoons sugar
- ¾ teaspoon ground ginger
- ¼ teaspoon cinnamon
- 1 teaspoon baking powder
- ½ teaspoon baking soda
- ⅛ teaspoon salt
- 1 egg
- ¼ cup molasses
- ½ cup buttermilk
- 2 tablespoons oil
- 1 teaspoon pure vanilla extract

Directions:

1. Preheat the toaster oven to 330°F.
2. Spray 6 x 6-inch baking dish lightly with cooking spray.
3. In a medium bowl, mix together all the dry ingredients.
4. In a separate bowl, beat the egg. Add molasses, buttermilk, oil, and vanilla and stir until well mixed.
5. Pour liquid mixture into dry ingredients and stir until well blended.
6. Pour batter into baking dish and Air-fry at 330°F for 20 minutes or until toothpick inserted in center of loaf comes out clean.

Easy Churros

Servings: 12

Cooking Time: 10 Minutes

Ingredients:

- ½ cup Water
- 4 tablespoons (¼ cup/½ stick) Butter
- ¼ teaspoon Table salt
- ½ cup All-purpose flour
- 2 Large egg(s)
- ¼ cup Granulated white sugar
- 2 teaspoons Ground cinnamon

Directions:

1. Bring the water, butter, and salt to a boil in a small saucepan set over high heat, stirring occasionally.

2. When the butter has fully melted, reduce the heat to medium and stir in the flour to form a dough. Continue cooking, stirring constantly, to dry out the dough until it coats the bottom and sides of the pan with a film, even a crust. Remove the pan from the heat, scrape the dough into a bowl, and cool for 15 minutes.

3. Using an electric hand mixer at medium speed, beat in the egg, or eggs one at a time, until the dough is smooth and firm enough to hold its shape.

4. Mix the sugar and cinnamon in a small bowl. Scoop up 1 tablespoon of the dough and roll it in the sugar mixture to form a small, coated tube about ½ inch in diameter and 2 inches long. Set it aside and make 5 more tubes for the small batch or 11 more for the large one.

5. Set the tubes on a plate and freeze for 20 minutes. Meanwhile, preheat the toaster oven to 375°F.

6. Set 3 frozen tubes in the air fryer oven for a small batch or 6 for a large one with as much air space between them as possible. Air-fry undisturbed for 10 minutes, or until puffed, brown, and set.

7. Use kitchen tongs to transfer the churros to a wire rack to cool for at least 5 minutes. Meanwhile, air-fry and cool the second batch of churros in the same way.

Printed by Libri Plureos GmbH in Hamburg,
Germany